Talk that Book!

Booktalks to Promote Reading

By Carol Littlejohn

PROFESSIONAL GROWTH SERIES®

A Publication of THE BOOK REPORT & LIBRARY TALK
Professional Growth Series

Linworth Publishing, Inc.
Worthington, Ohio

Published by Linworth Publishing, Inc.
480 East Wilson Bridge Road, Suite L
Worthington, Ohio 43085

Copyright©1999 by Linworth Publishing, Inc.

Series Information:
        From The Professional Growth Series

ISBN 0-938865-75-7

5 4 3 2 1

Table of Contents

Table of Contents continued

Table of Contents continued

Table of Contents continued

Table of Contents continued

Table of Contents continued

Table of Contents continued

Table of Contents continued

Introduction

Booktalking is a brief "commercial" of a book, giving just enough information to promote reading the book. Like any advertisement, you should have a "catchy" beginning and a cliffhanger ending so the audience remembers the book long after you have gone. Throughout the years I have written and performed booktalks in schools and libraries, and at book fairs and conferences. This is my opportunity to share these with you.

Some years ago a teacher asked me to booktalk to a group of students. Luckily, I had recently attended a local workshop on booktalking and wanted to give it a try. After my presentation I was surrounded by students with questions about other books and authors. That presentation made me a believer.

Over the years I discovered some benefits to writing booktalks. For example, I learned that I could remember the books years later. Taking the time to write booktalks etched the plot and characters vividly in my mind. If I needed to recall a book, I could go back to my written booktalk and easily refresh my memory.

I also learned that writing booktalks is an inexpensive way to introduce books to readers. You don't need equipment that may or may not work. All you need is the book to be available to the readers.

Booktalks can be used in a variety of ways, and they can be used at a variety of school functions. During any reading incentive programs, booktalks are useful to introduce the books to the readers. Booktalks also can be used to introduce a book to discussion groups.

All the booktalks discussed in this book have been used either in a classroom or library, or at a conference. A booktalk is successful only if the audience expresses enthusiasm about the book. Many of the booktalks in this book were rewritten after receiving an indifferent response. From experience, I've discovered if a booktalk doesn't work, discard the booktalk. Don't discard the book. Approach the book from another point of view and see if that gives more vitality to the booktalk.

In this collection I recommend books that are recently published as well as books that have endured the test of time. As I'm writing, all the recommended books are currently in print, but in-print status is subject to change. If a book is out of print, don't despair because many out-of-print books can be obtained through Internet and mail-order companies. Sometimes books are reprinted by publishing companies if there seems to be an interest. However, don't recommend a book that is not available to the audience. A booktalk without the book is similar to supplying people with a menu without the food available for them.

The booktalks are separated into three age groups: elementary (grades 4-6); middle school (grades 6-8); high school (grades 9-adults). These are not rigid categories, and certainly some readers will enjoy some books that are not in their category. In Chapters 2, 3, and 4, the booktalks are in alphabetical order by the author's last name. The ISBN numbers are not included because many books have different editions. In Chapter 5, "The Latest and the Greatest: Booktalking Best-sellers," I combined the most recent best-sellers into one program to demonstrate how to link the booktalks. The appendix contains an extensive index by titles, authors, genres, and subjects.

Feel free to skim and browse this book to see which titles interest you. These booktalks may inspire you to read some of the books. After all, that's the point of booktalks.

Let's talk those books!

ABOUT THE AUTHOR

Carol Littlejohn has been a young adult and children's librarian since completing her master's degree in Library Science in 1974. She has worked in college, public, and school libraries. Her last assignment was at the American International School of Johannesburg in South Africa. She is currently a library consultant and is developing a Web site for reading enthusiasts.

She has published articles about booktalking in *The Book Report, Library Talk, JOYS, VOYA, The ALAN Review,* and *Bookbird.* She also speaks to various organizations about reading and writing booktalks.

ACKNOWLEDGMENTS

Everyone thanks his or her family, but in this case I must acknowledge my family's immense contributions with their encouragement, support, and skills, which range from proofreading to downloading files. Thanks, Mike ("LJ"), Karl, and Drew! You guys made this project fun.

Others have contributed to my work and booktalks, even though they may not have realized their positive effect on me: the staff at Linworth Publishing, especially Carol Simpson, Carolyn Hamilton, and Marlene Woo-Lun; booktalkers Joni Bodart and Patrick Jones; colleagues and friends Professor Magdaleen Bester and Professor Pieter Van Brakel from Rand Africaans University in South Africa; Cathy Thomas; Nikki Fieser; Jeanette Gerlach; Anitra Lahey; Marjorie Van Heerdon; Sue McMurray; Cynthia Richey; Professor Doris Dale; the staff of the Shaler North Hills Library in Pittsburgh; and the teachers and students of the American International School in Johannesburg, especially Margie Bragg, Wendy Cresswell, Kate Fleming Baker, Susan Castaneda, Christine Grady Shereston, and Debbie Noils.

To all booktalkers, let's keep talking that book!

This book is dedicated to my mother,
Mary Veach Thomas.

Talk that Book Off the Shelves: Tips and Strategies

▶ PURPOSE OF BOOKTALKS

Booktalking is the most effective way to move books off the shelves and into the hands of readers. Think of yourself as a salesperson selling the love of reading. The booktalk is the advertisement, the book is the product, and the reader is the consumer. If a booktalk is successful, the reader will enthusiastically consume the book.

Booktalking can provide a link to other reading incentive programs. Some programs can be intimidating to reluctant readers. The student may be overwhelmed by selecting a book to read. Booktalks can help in narrowing a student's book selection choices.

Once the book is selected, that book will elicit a response from the reader. In the landmark book *Literature as Exploration* (Modern Language Association, 1938), educator Louise Rosenblatt theorizes that a reader brings an emotional history to a book. Rosenblatt compares it to hearing a symphony: Each person will respond differently to a piece of music, depending on knowledge and personal history. As booktalkers, we may not know which books

will provoke a positive response, but we can expose readers to a wide range of books. Then we step back and leave the choice to the reader.

Still, this observation is based upon personal experience. Unfortunately, not enough research has been done on booktalking. Joni Bodart was the first to do exploratory research on booktalking, but many questions still remain unresolved. Put simply, we know booktalking works, but we're not certain how. Until we know, our reward will come from readers' positive comments. Luckily, the result usually is immediate and gratifying.

▶ BOOKTALKS, BOOKTALKING, AND BOOKTALKERS

Everyone recommends a book now and then. However, that's not a booktalk, that's talking about a book. A *booktalk* is a written presentation of the book, reflecting its uniqueness and vividness.

Booktalking is a verbal presentation of selected books, usually to an audience.

Booktalkers present prepared booktalks in a relaxed and entertaining style. Like all storytellers, booktalkers' presentations reflect their background and personality. What works for one person may not be useful to someone else. It takes booktalking experience to discover what works.

▶ WAYS TO USE BOOKTALKS EFFECTIVELY

If you are a school media specialist, you are fortunate to have an audience that you will know over the years. Try to integrate booktalks into classes at least twice a year. Order several paperback copies of the books that you will use. Booktalk your favorite "shelf sitters" to get those books moving. Give the students a booklist of the books discussed, along with any other recommended titles. Keep an accurate list of students who request a book. Create a book display of favorites. If there is interest, start a book discussion group and booktalk books its members might enjoy.

Teachers can use booktalks in a variety of ways. Occasionally booktalk some books in the classroom library. Invite students to booktalk their favorites. Display booktalks on bulletin boards. Run trivia contests by giving the booktalk and requesting the title. During breaks, give brief booktalks. Surround the classroom with books and the love of reading.

If you are a public librarian, you may need to find an audience. You can either begin a book discussion group at your library or establish contacts with the local schools. Even if the school librarian booktalks, students and teachers occasionally like to hear a different voice and approach. Get to know the school librarian and principal, and ask them to recommend a convenient time to booktalk. Don't give up if the administrators say the teachers are too busy for booktalks. With

> **If you are a school media specialist, you are fortunate to have an audience that you will know over the years. Try to integrate booktalks into classes at least twice a year.**

polite pressure from you, they will agree. Then do such a good job at booktalking, they have to ask you back!

▶ BOOKTALKER RESOURCES

Booktalkers need a collection of booktalks selected from a variety of sources. Begin by selecting some booktalks from this book that suit your style. Photocopy these booktalks and begin a booktalk organizer. This organizer will save you time later.

Try to collect booktalks from other sources, as well. Look for books or articles by Joni Bodart, Hazel Rochman, Patrick Jones, Nancy Polette, and John Gillespie. These and other recommended books are at the end of the chapter. Also recommended is the Web site Booktalks: Quick and Simple (www.concord. k12.nh.us/ schools/rundlett/booktalk/). Other Web sites will be available in the future. Do online searches using keywords *"book talks"* (two words, enclosed in quotation marks) or *booktalks* (one word, no quotation marks). These booktalks will go into your organizer as well.

You will also need to know the best-sellers and latest award-winning books. Magazines such as *The Book Report, Library Talk, VOYA* (Voice of Youth Advocates), *Book Links, JOYS* (Journal of Youth Services), and *School Library Journal* recommend young adult and children's books.

Some Web sites will provide you with the latest booklists. Try David Brown's The Children's Literature Guide (www.ucalgary. ca/~dkbrown/index.html), Fairrosa's CyberLibrary (www.users.interport.net/~fairrosa/), Carol Hurst's Children's Literature Site (www.crocker.com/~rbotis/), Kathy Schrock's Guide for Educators (www.capecod.net/ schrockguide/index.htm), Kay E. Vandergrift's

Special Interest Page (www.sclis.rutgers.edu/special.kay/kayhp2.html), and the American Library Association Web site (www.ala.org).

▷ THE BOOKTALK ORGANIZER

As your booktalks accumulate, you will need a sturdy box to file booktalks. For easy access, booktalks should be filed alphabetically by the author's last name.

The back of the booktalk can be used to give vital information about the presentation. After the booktalk, make a notation of the date, grade, and school of the presentation. This prevents any repetition of booktalks. If a booktalk goes over well, you can place a "star" on the back. That booktalk may open the program next time. If the book is circulated immediately after the talk, place a "check mark" on the booktalk.

With some effort, the booktalk organizer becomes a record of past booktalks and a resource for future presentations. If you record the response of the booktalks, this information will add to the success of the next booktalk.

▷ WRITING BOOKTALKS

You may find that you are better at writing your booktalks because your writing will be closer to your speaking style. Try it and see what happens.

I find it most effective to write a booktalk immediately after reading the book. The details of the book are still vivid and, hopefully, the book's appeal generates an enthusiastic response.

Your writing style can vary from booktalk to booktalk. You might attempt to write booktalks in the style of the author. If the book is written from the main character's point of view, you can try the first-person viewpoint. Other times you could pretend to interview the main character. Sometimes you can write the booktalk as an excerpt from a diary.

Give enough information about the book to excite the reader without revealing the ending. Begin a booktalk with some kind of "hook," using either a question or intriguing statement. Try to repeat the book title and author at the end of each booktalk so the audience can remember the book.

After you finish writing your booktalk, add your booktalk to your booktalk organizer. Put your initials on the booktalk to indicate your authorship. With many booktalks accumulated over time, authorship can be difficult to recall.

> Give enough information about the book to excite the reader without revealing the ending. Begin a booktalk with some kind of "hook," using either a question or intriguing statement.

▷ BOOKTALKING PRESENTATIONS

Begin your presentation with a winner so you can capture the audience's interest. Once you have experience, you can use a booktalk that has already received a positive response.

As you continue your presentation, be flexible to the needs of the audience. Size up the group and quickly determine their reading interests. Let them tell you which of the books on display interest them. Begin with those books and then gradually bring up others that are different. The nonverbal members of the group may have different reading interests.

Spend about one to three minutes on each book, giving just enough time to give the book a "personality." Try to provide transitions between books. You might say, "Here's another mystery you might like," then go right into the booktalk. (See page 133, "The Latest and the Greatest: Booktalking Best-sellers," for an example of transitions between books.) You usually can booktalk 10 or 20 titles within 30 minutes.

Bring more books than you think you will need. You may require them, and, regardless, this demonstrates your enthusiasm for reading.

Someone may ask about a book you have not enjoyed. My answer is usually, "I'm glad you enjoyed reading it." Try not to downgrade someone else's reading habits or tastes. Studies indicate that reading interests can change. By negating someone's reading tastes, you may keep that person from reading. After all, reading is the main purpose behind booktalks.

▶ BOOKTALKING DEBATE: IS MEMORIZATION REQUIRED?

Many booktalkers do memorize booktalks. However, sometimes you may just be too busy to devote time to memorization.

There are some booktalking techniques that don't require memorization. One technique is to place the card of the booktalk behind the book. This "cheat sheet" is helpful because the audience focuses on the cover of the book rather than your card. Do try to make eye contact while reading, by giving a quick scan of a line and saying the line with your eyes on the audience.

Also, you can design or copy the book's cover with the title and author, and attach your booktalk on the back. You can then read the booktalk as they are looking over your book cover. For protection from wear and tear, laminate the book cover.

Sometimes you can booktalk without saying a word. Place the booktalks within books that are conveniently displayed, or display the booktalks on a bulletin board with the books underneath. You can complete another task and booktalk at the same time.

▶ EVALUATION OF BOOKTALKING

To evaluate the success of booktalking, listen to and observe the reactions of the audience. There will be an immediate response to any presentation. By careful observation, you can evaluate that response. For future reference, note reactions on each booktalk.

Remember, an audience's immediate reaction is to the booktalk, not the book. The reader may not respond positively to the actual book. Later, you will need to discover the reaction to the actual book. If possible, ask the reader to review the book. These quick questions are helpful: Would you recommend this book? Why or why not?

You might consider submitting a short, written survey to the group about their favorite books and authors, and their reading interests. Be prepared for some honest, even negative, answers. However, reasonable suggestions should be implemented so that the audience knows their opinions are respected and valued.

Of course, the best gauge of your success is to have someone express excitement about a book you recommended. This makes your effort worthwhile.

> There will be an immediate response to any presentation. By careful observation, you can evaluate that response.

▶ BIBLIOGRAPHY ON BOOKTALKING AND READING, CHAPTER 1

Bodart, Joni Richards, "Booktalks Do Work! The Effects of Booktalking on Attitude and Circulation." *Illinois Libraries*, June 1985, pp. 378-381.

Bodart, Joni Richards, editor, *Booktalking the Award Winners: Children's Retrospective Volume.* H. W. Wilson, 1997.

Bodart, Joni Richards, editor, *Booktalking the Award Winners: Young Adult Retrospective Volume.* H. W. Wilson, 1996.

Bodart, Joni Richards, *100 World-Class Thin Books or What to Read when Your Book Report Is Due Tomorrow!* Libraries Unlimited, 1993.

Gillespie, John T., and Diana L. Lembo, *Juniorplots: A Book Talk Manual for Teachers and Librarians.* R. R. Bowker, 1967. Also *Seniorplots* series.

Jones, Patrick, *Connecting Young Adults and Libraries: A How-To-Do It Manual.* 2nd ed. Neal Schuman, 1998.

Lomas, Mary Elizabeth, *To Choose or not to Choose: The Effect of Varied Influences on the Selection of Library Books by Junior High School Students.* Ph.D. dissertation. University of Nebraska, 1993.

Krashen Stephen, *The Power of Reading: Insights from the Research.* Libraries Unlimited, 1993.

Polette, Nancy, ed., *Novel Booktalks to Read and to Perform: Award Winners and Other Favorites.* Book Lures, 1994. Also, Volume 2.

Reeder, Gail, *Effect of Booktalks on Adolescent Reading.* Ph.D. dissertation. University of Nebraska, 1991.

Rochman, Hazel, *Against Borders: Promoting Books for a Multicultural World.* ALA Books, 1993.

Rochman, Hazel, *Tales of Love and Terror: Booktalking the Classics Old and New.* American Library Association, 1987.

Rosenblatt, Louise, *Literature as Exploration.* Modern Language Association, 1938.

Rosenblatt, L. M., *The Reader, the Text, the Poem: The Transactional Theory of the Literary Work.* Southern Illinois University, 1993. With a new preface and epilogue.

CHAPTER **2**

Booktalks for Elementary Schools (Grades 4-6)

These books are selected for the elementary school student because the books are free of sex, drugs, and obvious profanity. When recommending books to younger readers, we must be cautious of the content. At the same time we want to recommend books that are well written and provocative. These booktalks can be used with middle school readers, as well.

I have added information about literary awards, but I have not done an extensive search on this. The Newbery Award is awarded annually by the American Library Association for the best children's book by an American author. The Carnegie Award is awarded annually by The British Library Association for the best children's book by a British author. The Young Readers' Choice Award is given annually by young readers in the Northern United States and Canada. (I am interested in this one because readers from the fourth to eighth grades choose their favorite

book from a selected list. Young readers seem to like these selections.) The Coretta Scott King Award is given annually to an African-American author for an outstanding contribution to children's literature.

I have also noted whether a book is an excellent read-aloud choice. During convenient times, these books can be read chapter by chapter to a class. My suggestion is that you introduce the book with a booktalk and then begin reading the first chapter. You can also put these booktalks within the books of the classroom library. Many of the fourth grade students will be able to read them.

Some of my comments will suggest books in a particular genre. For example, some younger students will not be able handle horror, while others will embrace it. For this reason, I have included some harmless horror for students intrigued with the *Goosebumps* or *Cliffhangers* series.

Atwater, Richard & Florence.
Mr. Popper's Penguins.
Illustrated by Robert Lawson.
Little, Brown, 1939, 139pp.
Grades 3-5.
A Newbery Honor book.

Humor. *Animals (penguins); ecology; show business; work.*

"Hello, Mr. Popper in Stillwater at 432 Proudfoot Avenue. This is Admiral Drake from the South Pole. Thanks for your nice letter. Watch for a surprise."

That radio broadcast caught the Poppers by surprise. But nothing like the surprise that occurred when the large package arrived. The box read "unpack at once" and "keep cool." Inside was a live penguin! Mr. Popper loved this penguin on sight and called him Captain Cook.

Where will Captain Cook live? In the refrigerator. What does Captain Cook eat? A live goldfish. How do you take a penguin for a walk? Very, very carefully. How do you cure Captain Cook of loneliness? By adding more penguins until a dozen penguins occupy the Popper house. How do you pay for the upkeep of all these penguins? Send the penguins on tour, of course.

"Ladies and gentlemen, live on stage, *Mr. Popper's Penguins!*"

Avi. **The Barn.**
Orchard Books, 1994,
106pp. Grades 5 & Up.

Historical fiction. *Death; illness (physical); pioneer life; responsibility.*

Note: This brief yet brilliant novel is deceptive because the author discusses the complex topic of death. You might suggest the book to teachers as a read-aloud.

"Your father has met with an accident."

Those words changed my life forever. In 1855 I left school to come home to help my family. My father, brother, and sister live with me on a homestead in Yamhill County, Oregon. My father has palsy and just lies in bed staring at the walls. He is like a vegetable, but he's alive. We are grateful for that.

Then I got an idea. A barn! We would build a barn for Father, and he would get well. It would work. I knew it would.

Later, I needed to know the answers to some important questions: Did we build the barn for me? Did we build the barn for Father? Did Father get me to build it for all of us?

Maybe, just maybe, it was all these things.

Avi. **Devil's Race.**
HarperTrophy, 1986,
152pp. Grades 5 & Up.

Horror. *Occult; responsibility; revenge; supernatural.*

There are two John Prouds. One is alive. The other has been dead for hundreds of years, hanged for being a demon.

The living John Proud is drawn to the grave of the dead John Proud. The grave is of John Proud's great-great-great-great grandfather, who is buried near Devil's Race. Devil's Race is a high creek in an area considered haunted.

John IV must face certain things in himself. Does his ancestor possess his mind and body? Is the spirit of the demon inside him?

Enter the Devil's Race as John races with his devil.

Avi. The Fighting Ground. (Pbk.)
HarperTrophy, 1984,
157pp. Grades 4-6.

Historical fiction. *American Revolutionary War; responsibility; rites of passage; war.*

On April 3, 1778, during the American Revolutionary War, 13-year-old Jonathan goes through the most harrowing 24 hours of his life. At the beginning of that unforgettable day, Jonathan thinks war is noble and fun. He foolishly joins a Patriot regiment and is captured by German mercenaries called Hessians. By the end of the day, he realizes how his handicapped father must have suffered. Now Jonathan recognizes the futility of war.

Will Jonathan make it home? Find out in *The Fighting Ground.*

Avi. Something Upstairs: A Tale of Ghosts. Orchard Books, 1988, 116pp. Grades 4-7.

Horror. *Occult; revenge; suicide; supernatural; time travel; trust.*

I'm Avi, author of *Something Upstairs: A Tale of Ghosts.* I often visit schools to talk about books and to talk to young people.

During one of my school visits, I met Kenny Huldorf. Kenny told me this amazing story about a ghost named Caleb who lived upstairs in a historic house that the Huldorfs had just bought. Many years ago Caleb had been murdered, and he wanted Kenny to help him discover the murderer.

Get ready for the scare of your life.

Avi. The True Confessions of Charlotte Doyle.
Illustrated by Ruth E. Murray.
Orchard Books, 1990, 224pp.
Grades 4 & Up.
A Newbery Honor book.

Historical fiction. *Class conflict; revenge; responsibility.*

Note: If you like, find a torn or antique-looking diary, place this booktalk inside and read in a British accent.

"Don't board that ship, Miss," warns Charlotte Doyle's lawyer and family friend. "'Tis not safe for a young girl to sail the *Seahawk* for 'tis haunted with legendary tales of death and mutiny!"

"I must board this ship," protests 13-year-old Charlotte. "My family is expecting me in America. They will think I'm dead or sick if I do not board."

Thus, on June 16, 1832, Charlotte Doyle boards the *Seahawk* in Liverpool, England. To her surprise, she discovers she is the only passenger. All the other passengers refused to board when they learned the ship was the bewitched *Seahawk.*

To Charlotte's horror, she discovers the crew is seeking revenge on Captain Jaggery because he chopped off the arm of a crewman on an earlier voyage. Mutiny is certain. What is not certain is what will happen to Charlotte among these anarchists. Should she befriend the friendly captain or give her allegiance to the suspicious crew?

Babbitt, Natalie.
The Devil's Storybook. (Pbk.)
Sunburst/Farrar, Strauss & Giroux,
1993, 101pp. Grades 4 & Up.

Short stories. *Ethics; magic; revenge; supernatural.*

I usually choose the story "Wishes" and read it to the audience.

Did you know the devil can tell stories? And what a story-teller! Of course, the devil tries to stir up trouble for all us humans. The devil tries to make us do all the wrong things.

Try these humorous stories from *The Devil's Storybook*.

Babbitt, Natalie.
Tuck Everlasting.
Farrar, Strauss & Giroux,
1975, 139pp. Grades 4 & Up.

Fantasy. *Aging; death; magic; secrets; supernatural.*

This classic novel is a recommended read-aloud. The author uses analogies, such as the changing seasons, to portray the revolving cycles of life.

Would you like to live forever? Sounds great, doesn't it? Think about it.

The Tuck family drank from a magical spring and were granted eternal life. Jesse Tuck has been 17 for 87 years! Of course, the Tuck family–Mae, Tuck, Miles, and Jesse–cannot live in the same place year after year. People would get older while the Tucks would remain the same. The Tucks can never make friends. They have only each other for the rest of their lives–forever!

Winnie Foster discovers the Tucks' secret of immortality, but she promises not to tell. Unfortunately, the man in the yellow suit has also discovered the secret. He plans to sell this potion for immortality to the world. How can he be stopped?

Banks, Lynne Reid.
One More River.
Avon Books, 1992, 246pp.
Grades 5 & Up. Glossary of Hebrew and Yiddish words.

Historical fiction. *Jews; Middle East; rites of passage; war; work.*

This book has significant changes in the various editions.
This 1992 edition is more acceptable for fifth and sixth graders.

"We're moving to Israel, Lesley. Canada isn't our country, not really. It's a Christian country. We're Jews. We're moving. Accept it."

Lesley must reluctantly say goodbye to her friends and to her older brother Noah. Noah hasn't seen their parents since he married a Catholic, but Lesley secretly keeps in touch with him. Surprisingly, Noah thinks that Lesley's moving to Israel is a good idea.

At first Lesley hates Israel and living on a kibbutz. There is no privacy. Daily lessons are taught in Hebrew. After her lessons, she must do two hours of farm work. At the end of a long day, she has only a short time to visit her parents. Then she goes back to the room she shares with three roommates–one of them a boy!

Lesley loves to escape to the bank of the Jordan River to collect her thoughts. She notices a young Arab boy on the other bank. "He's our enemy," her friend Shula tells her. Nevertheless, Lesley would wave to the boy and he would return the greeting.

When the Six Day War occurs, Lesley has to reevaluate this friendship with the Arab boy. Is he a friend or enemy?

Bellairs, John. The House with a Clock in Its Walls. (Pbk.) Dial, 1973, 179pp. Grades 5 & Up. First in a series: **The Figure in the Shadows** and **The Letter, the Witch and the Ring** follow.

Horror. *End-of-the-world; magic; occult; supernatural.*

Tick, tick, tick.

Every night Lewis and his Uncle Jonathan could hear the ticking of a clock. The clock is inside the walls of an old house with secret passageways and dozens of unused, unexplored rooms. This clock is different from any other clock because, when it stops ticking, the world will end!

The magical clock was placed inside the walls of the house by a previous owner, the evil sorcerer Isaac Izard. Now Lewis and his wizard of an uncle must stop that clock without destroying it.

Can Lewis and his uncle Jonathan find the clock and reverse its spell? Hurry and read this thriller because time is running out in *The House with a Clock in Its Walls*!

Blume, Judy. Freckle Juice. Illustrated by Sonia O. Lisker. Dell, 1971, 46pp. Grades 3-5.

Humor. *School; self-identity.*

Andrew Marcus wants freckles. Freckles are a good thing to have. For one thing, no one will notice if your neck is dirty. Then you don't have to wash as much.

Nicky Lane has freckles, about a million of them. When Andrew asked Nicky how he got his freckles, Nicky says, "Are you kidding? I was born with them. Whatta you think?"

Andrew felt stupid. Luckily, Sharon, the class snoop, overheard and promised Andrew that for 50 cents, she would give him freckle juice. Then Andrew could have a million freckles, like Nicky, or only six freckles, like Sharon.

Will the freckle juice work?

Blume, Judy. Tales of a Fourth Grade Nothing. Illustrated by Roy Doty. Bantam Doubleday Dell, 1972, 120pp. Grades 4-6. First in a series: **Fudge-a-mania** and **Superfudge** follow. A Young Readers' Choice Award winner.

Humor. *Family; responsibility; rivalry; self-identity.*

Note: Elementary students love this series. Teachers can use this as a read-aloud and librarians can read one chapter as an introduction. One minor character, Sheila, takes the lead in Blume's **Otherwise Known as Sheila the Great.**

My mother isn't my biggest problem. Okay, she's a cleanliness freak. She makes me crazy sometimes, making me wash my hands with soap. That's no big deal.

My dad isn't my biggest problem either. He watches commercials all day because he's in advertising. That's okay with me.

Nope, my biggest problem is my brother, Farley Drexel Hatcher. We call him Fudge. I don't know which name is worse. Since Fudge is only two years old, he doesn't care what he's called as long as he gets his way.

Whether he's messing up my homework, trying to fly on a jungle gym or giving himself a haircut, he is a big pain. When Fudge eats my pet turtle Dribble, that's the last straw!

I'm tired of being a fourth grade nothing. How can I get Mom and Dad to pay attention to me for a change?

Brink, Carol Ryrie.
Caddie Woodlawn.
Illustrated by Trina Schart Hyman.
Macmillan, 1935, 242pp.
Grades 4-6.
A Newbery Award winner.

Historical fiction. *Family; Native Americans; pioneer life; rites of passage; women's issues.*

 Note: This is a good one for fans of Laura Ingall Wilder's Little House series.

"I wish mother would let me wear boy's clothes," Caddie Woodlawn complained to her brothers.

Life was too exciting to be a girl in 1864 in the woods of western Wisconsin. Free-spirited Caddie Woodlawn hunted, fished, and explored with her brothers Tom and Warren. Caddie left "women's work" to her mother and sisters.

Caddie even made friends with Indian John, who called her "Missee Red Hair." Once Caddie even saved Indian John's life. The settlers had heard rumors that there was to be an Indian attack. The Woodlawns didn't believe it because they respected Indian John and his tribe.

One day Caddie overheard some settlers planning to attack the Indians first. Caddie saddled her horse Betsy and rode to the camp to warn Indian John. Indian John promised to move the camp to avoid war.

This story is true. How do I know this? Caddie Woodlawn was the author's grandmother.

Brink, Carol Ryrie. **The Pink Motel.**
(Pbk.) Aladdin/Macmillan, 1993,
214pp. Grades 4-6.

Mysteries/thrillers. *Interracial relations; responsibility; work.*

Until Kirby Mellon was 10, nothing very exciting had happened to him or his little sister, Bitsy.

Then, suddenly, Kirby's mother inherited a motel, and things began to happen. Mind you, it wasn't just any motel. It was a hot pink motel, the perfect place for adventure.

The action in the Pink Motel never stops. Excitement intensifies with alligator hunting, dognapping, and searching for Great-Granduncle Hiram's secret treasure. The guests in the Pink Motel are wonderfully wacky, too: a magician from The World, a carpenter from Nobody Knows, and an artist from Greenwich Village.

Come on, book a room at *The Pink Motel.*

Bunting, Eve. **Coffin on a Case.**
(Pbk.) HarperTrophy, 1992, 105pp.
Grades 4-6. A Young Readers' Choice
Award winner.

Mysteries/thrillers. *Crime; survival.*

I'm Coffin. Henry Coffin. No, I'm not a mortician who works on dead bodies. I'm a detective. That is, my Dad is a detective, but I help him whenever I'm not going to school or daydreaming.

I keep fantasizing about a gorgeous babe coming into the detective agency asking for help. That's what happens in the movies, right?

Like the movies, it happens to me. A beauty named Lily Larson asks for help in locating her mother, who has disappeared for the fourth time.

Okay, Lily Larson, step aside, your troubles are over. Coffin is on the case!

Bunting, Eve. **Nasty, Stinky Sneakers.** HarperCollins, 1994, 104pp. Grades 4-6.

Humor. *Peer pressure; revenge; school.*

Colin owns a pair of nasty, stinky sneakers. His sneakers smell so bad that his mom makes him leave them outside the apartment. His sneakers smell so bad that his sister's hamster drops, gasping, to the bottom of its cage. His sneakers smell so bad that he plans to enter them into the Stinkiest Sneakers in the World Contest.

Unfortunately, someone has stolen Colin's sneakers. Is it Jack Dunn, who plans to enter his own stinky sneakers in the contest? Is it Mr. Sebastian, a neighbor who complained about the smell?

Sneakers are not the only thing Colin smells. He smells a rat!

Bunting, Eve. **SOS Titanic.** (Pbk.) Scholastic, 1996, 246pp. Grades 4-8.

Historical fiction. *Class conflict; death; Ireland; responsibility; rivalry; survival.*

Note: All ages seem to enjoy books that involve a huge disaster like the sinking of the Titanic. This book is appropriate for the younger readers.

"I have a question for ya. Can ya swim?" Jonnie Flynn smirked at Barry as the *Titanic* left Ireland, bound for New York.

Barry swallowed hard. He didn't want to leave his grandparents and travel alone. Barry especially didn't want to face the Flynn family by himself. Jonnie and Frank hated Barry. Barry knew they would bully him on this trip. Luckily, Barry would sail first class and the Flynns would be in steerage. Maybe Barry could avoid them.

When the *Titanic* hit an iceberg, Barry no longer cared about the past. Besides, Barry rather liked Pegeen Flynn, their older sister. All the Flynns were trapped behind gates with the other steerage passengers. How could Barry help all of them escape?

Burch, Robert. **Ida Early Comes Over the Mountain.** Viking, 1980, 145pp. Grades 4-6. First in a series: **Merry Christmas, Ida Early** follows.

Humor. *Ethics; peer pressure; responsibility.*

"Howdy, one and all!"

Ida Early comes over the mountain like a house afire. Once Ida Early becomes the Suttons' housekeeper, nothing is ever the same again.

Dressed like a man in her bulging overalls, Ida claims she was once a lion tamer, a cook on a pirate ship, and a stunt pilot. Who knows if Ida is telling a whopper? One thing is for certain–Ida Early is a barrel of laughs.

Butterworth, Oliver.
The Enormous Egg.
Illustrated by Louis Darling.
Little, Brown, 1986.
First published in 1954. Grades 4-6.

Humor. *Animals (dinosaurs); crime; politics; responsibility; science.*

My name is Nate Twitchell, but I can't help that. I live in Freedom, New Hampshire, but I can't help that either. I want to tell you about this amazing thing that happened that changed my life.

One of our hens laid an enormous egg with a leathery shell. The egg measured almost a foot and a half around and weighed over three pounds. I know these facts because some reporters from the *Christian Science Monitor* wrote about the egg.

When the enormous egg hatched, it was a little dinosaur! A triceratops, to be exact. I named the dinosaur Uncle Beasley.

My friend Dr. Ziemer suggested that I bring Uncle Beasley to Washington, D.C., to the National Museum. He thought I should stay around and take care of Uncle Beasley because the dinosaur might cause some problems. Boy, was he right. Uncle Beasley grew to be over 20 feet tall and that became one big problem.

When Uncle Beasley caused some terrible traffic jams during his daily walks, the politicians raised a terrible ruckus. Senator Granderson wanted to stop Uncle Beasley right in his dinosaur tracks. Will Senator Granderson succeed in getting rid of Uncle Beasley?

Byars, Betsy. **The Dark Stairs.**
Viking, 1994, 130pp. Grades 4-6.
First in the Herculeah Jones mystery series: **Tarot Says Beware; Dead Letter; Death's Door;** and **Disappearing Acts** follow.

Mysteries/thrillers. *Crime; survival.*

For those readers who like the Nancy Drew or Hardy Boys series, this series is also recommended.

That unlucky day, Friday the 13th, was the day the mystery began for Herculeah Jones. She spotted her dad, a police officer, looking for a prowler at Dead Oaks, a spooky old house. Her mother, a private detective, was interviewing a guy that looked an escapee from a zombie movie.

Herculeah decided to investigate Dead Oaks herself. She crept inside the dark, sinister basement to investigate. Within minutes the "zombie" arrived.

Herculeah froze. She heard the sound of hammering. The "zombie" was nailing the door shut! And she was trapped inside.

Carlson, Natalie Savage. **The Family Under the Bridge.** Illustrated by Garth Williams. Scholastic, 1958, 97pp. A Newbery Honor book.

Historical fiction. *Europe (France); homeless; responsibility.*

"Your fortune, monsieur," said a musical voice. "You will meet with adventure today."

Armand looked carefully at the gypsy. Every day was an adventure. Armand kept everything he owned in an old baby buggy and pushed it on the streets of Paris. That was plenty of adventure for an old hobo.

However, the gypsy was right. Armand met three redheaded children who stole his heart. Suzy, Paul, and Evelyne Calcet want two things for Christmas: to stay together as a family and to have a home.

What will happen to this homeless family who lives under a bridge?

Choi, Sook Nyul. **The Year of Impossible Goodbyes.** (Pbk.) Dell, 1993. Grades 5-8. First in a series: **Echoes of a White Giraffe** and **A Gathering of Pearls** follow.

Historical fiction. *Asia (Korea); homeless; responsibility; survival; World War II.*

I have placed the second and third book of the series on pages 50-51 because Sookan enters her adolescence and has a romance. Many students enjoy this series.

In the year of impossible goodbyes, 10-year-old Sookan must say goodbye to her country, her family, and her way of life.

During World War II, North Korea is occupied by the Japanese. After the war, North Korea is occupied by the Russians. Sookan can not decide which captors are more cruel. The Japanese are disdainful of the Koreans and torture them mercilessly with beatings and killings. At first the Russians seem to be nicer, but they have secret police who round up prisoners late at night to torture or kill them.

Sookan, her mother and her younger brother try the best way they can to endure the cruelties. Sookan's mother manages a sock factory for the Japanese. When she becomes ill, she is taken away by the Japanese, leaving Sookan and her younger brother with their Aunt Tiger.

Can Sookan locate her mother and make a new life?

Christopher, John. **When the Tripods Came.** Macmillan, 1973, 151 pp. Grades 5 & Up. First in a series: **The White Mountains; The City of Gold and Lead;** and **The Pool of Fire** follow.

Science fiction. *End-of-the-world; ethics; friendship; responsibility; sports; survival; war.*

Middle school readers will like this series, as well.

When the Tripods came, nothing was ever the same again.

These mechanical monsters from another world have taken all the Earthlings as their slaves. Correction: Not all the Earthlings are slaves, only the Earthlings who wear the aliens' metal caps on their heads.

However, all Earthlings from the White Mountains are uncapped. Thirteen-year-old Will and his friend Fritz plot to overthrow the Tripods by entering the Games, which are similar to the Olympics. All Game winners are sent to the City as slaves to the Tripods.

How can Will and Fritz destroy the Tripods? Try this series by John Christopher about life on Earth *After the Tripods Came.*

Cohen, Barbara. **Thank You, Jackie Robinson.** Illustrations by Richard Cuffari. (Pbk.) Scholastic, 1989, 126 pp. Grades 4-6.

Sports. *African Americans; interracial relations; illness (physical); men's issues; racism; sports (baseball).*

Some students may be unaware that African Americans were denied certain careers in 1947. This book would be an excellent read-aloud to a class.

The year is 1947. Times were different then. The baseball team the Dodgers were in Brooklyn with a new team member: Jackie Robinson. He is the first African American to play in a major league.

Sam Green doesn't care about that. He just loves the Brooklyn Dodgers, especially Jackie Robinson. Sam has never seen the Brooklyn Dodgers play. His mom is too busy running a restaurant and inn to take Sam to a baseball game.

Then Sam meets Davy, an African-American cook in his mom's restaurant. Davy loves Jackie Robinson just as much as Sam does. Best of all, he wants to take Sam with him to all the Brooklyn Dodgers games. How great can it be?

However, something happens to Sam's new friend that changes their lives forever. The only person who can fix the problem is the legendary Jackie Robinson. Will he help two of his biggest fans?

Cooper, Susan. **The Boggart.**
Random House, 1993, 182pp.
Grades 4 & Up. First in a series: **The Boggart and the Monster** follows.

Horror. *Computers; occult; supernatural.*

Note: This book combines folklore and the supernatural in a light, entertaining way. The computer also plays a prominent role, which gives the book a contemporary twist.

Beware of the boggart! The boggart is an ancient mysterious spirit who plays many tricks like a mischievous kid.

The Volnik family had never heard of a boggart until they inherited a Scottish castle and accidentally brought a boggart back to Canada with them. Believe it or not, the boggart is trapped within the family's computer!

What should Emily and Jessup do? Should they delete the supernatural spirit or download it back to Scotland? What would you do?

Coville, Bruce. **The Dragonslayers.**
Illustrated by Katherine Coville. Pocket Books, 1994, 119pp. Grades 4-7.

Fantasy. *Magic; occult; rites of passages; rivalry; supernatural; women's issues.*

"My kingdom is filled with fools and cowards. I'll give half my kingdom for a knight with some courage." King Mildred fumes. "Yes, I'll give half my kingdom and my daughter's hand in marriage to whomever slays the wicked dragon!"

"Not if I get there first," mutters Princess Willie. She has no intention of living a quiet royal life. She wants to be a knight!

Princess Willie chops off her tresses, dons a suit of armor, and sets off for the Forest of Wonder. She meets two other Dragonslayers, Elizar and his squire, Brian. Can they stop arguing long enough to face the battle with the dragon?

Creech, Sharon. **Walk Two Moons.**
(Pbk.) Macmillan, 1994, 244pp.
Grades 5 & Up. A Newbery Award winner.

Realistic fiction. *Death; illness (physical); problem parents; trust.*

Note: You can write the three messages on stationery and present them one by one. Then go into the booktalk.

"Don't judge a man until you've walked two moons in his moccasins."

"Everyone has his own agenda."

"In the course of a lifetime, what does it matter?"

My best friend, Phoebe Winterbottom, sees these mysterious messages taped to her door. She thinks the notes are linked to her missing mother. I'm not so sure about that, but I do understand Phoebe's frustration. You see, my mother has also gone away and she won't be coming back.

I tell my grandparents all about my friend Phoebe and those strange messages. We're going on a long car trip to visit my mom. As we get closer and closer to our destination, I think about Phoebe's mom and my mom. Both disappeared without an adequate explanation. How could they do that to us?

Maybe we need to walk two moons in our moms' moccasins so we can understand and forgive.

Cross, Gillian. **The Great American Elephant Chase.** Holiday House, 1992, 193pp. Grades 4 & Up.

Adventure. *Animals (elephants); crime; homeless; pioneer life; revenge; runaways.*

Have you heard the joke about stealing an elephant?

"Hey, just where do you think you're going with that elephant?" shouts a police officer.

You look behind yourself, trying to cover the elephant with your body as you say, "What elephant?"

That's the predicament that Cissy and Tad encounter during the late 1800s. Just how do you hide an elephant from two conniving, ill-tempered varmints who claim Khush the elephant belongs to them? How do you hide something that attracts attention wherever it goes?

Cissy and Tad try to hide Khush by traveling down the Monongahela and Ohio rivers. Then they head up the Mississippi and Missouri rivers by foot, train, flatboat, and steamboat.

How do you hide an elephant? Very, very carefully.

Curtis, Christopher Paul. **The Watsons Go to Birmingham— 1963.** Delacorte, 1995, 210pp. Grades 4 & Up. A Newbery Honor book.

Historical fiction. *African Americans; death; family; men's issues; racism; responsibility; rites of passage.*

The Watsons are a riot.

In their neighborhood in Flint, Michigan, they are known as the "Weird Watsons." There's Byron, a 13-year-old hot shot. There's 10-year-old Kenny, who's called "Cockeyed Kenny" because of a lazy eye that won't move. There's also Momma, who's from Alabama. There's Dad, who teases Momma about the warm weather she left behind.

There are many stories about the Weird Watsons. Once Kenny was bothered by the bully Larry Dunn who liked to give something called the "Maytag wash." Larry liked to roll his victims in the snow! Byron took care of Larry by directing him in Byron's movie, *The Great Carp Escape.* Guess who played the lead role, Carp? Larry, of course. Byron chased that Carp all across the neighborhood.

Some stories are not humorous. When the Watsons go to Birmingham, they become part of civil rights history when four girls are killed by a bomb. Now the Watsons must accept that people hate them just because they are African Americans. That hatred can lead to murder.

Dahl, Roald. **Going Solo.** (Pbk.) Farrar, Strauss & Giroux, 1986, 210 pp. Grades 5 & Up. Second in a series: **Boy** precedes.

Biography. *Africa; men's issues; Middle East; survival; World War II.*

There are thrills and chills on every page of this autobiography by Roald Dahl. He solos in his Royal Air Force plane. He braves lions in eastern Africa. He demonstrates that his life was just as exciting as any of his books.

There are many stories. One is about the green mamba snake in East Africa. Roald spots the deadly snake sliding up the steps of an English family's house. He screams to the family to get out of the house. Then he runs to get the "Snake Man," a Scottish fellow who captures deadly snakes to send to zoos.

The Snake Man appears with a burlap bag and an eight-foot pole. Silently and methodically he captures and bags the snake. As the Snake Man leaves the house, he turns to Roald and sadly says, "Pity about the dog. You better get it out of the way before the children see it."

Dahl, Roald. The Witches.
Illustrated by Quentin Blake. (Pbk.)
Viking, 1983, 200pp. Grades 4-7.

Fantasy. *Magic; occult; revenge; secrets; supernatural; survival.*

Do you want to know how to spot a witch? She always wears gloves, even during summer, to hide her claws. She has large nostrils to smell children. The pupils in her eyes change color. Because she is bald, she wears a wig and is always scratching her head. Oh yes, she has a bluish tinge on her teeth because her saliva is blue.

One child spots a witch. He hides during a meeting of The Royal Society for Prevention of Cruelty to Children. He discovers that this organization is actually a group of witches plotting to turn all children into mice!

What if the witches smell him hiding behind the curtain? Would the witches change him into a mouse? You'd better believe it!

DeFelice, Cynthia. Lostman's River.
Atheneum Books for Young Readers, 1994, 160pp. Grades 4-7.

Realistic fiction. *Crime; ecology; ethics; problem parents; responsibility; rites of passage; substance abuse (alcohol).*

What was that stranger doing poling up Lostman's River to where we make our home?

My family don't trust strangers, not since we ran from New York to Florida over five years ago. My Pa had been accused of murdering Samuel Davenport. Pa had got drunk and then awakened next to a dead man. Pa don't recollect what happened, so he ran. We ran.

Them strangers that come to Lostman's River are running from the law, too. They want to kill the birds and alligators for money and they need us to help 'em through the deadly river.

Maybe we all need to learn to stop running and face our responsibilities. For instance, I seen a man murdered in cold blood. Do I report the murder to the law and risk exposing Pa?

DeFelice, Cynthia. Weasel. (Pbk.)
Macmillan, 1990, 128pp. Avon, 1991, 128pp. Grades 4-6.

Adventure. *Disability (physical); pioneer life; revenge; survival.*

Have you ever heard of the legendary killer Weasel?

Like the animal, Weasel hunts by night, sleeps by day, and kills for the sport of killing. The local legend says Weasel is part man and part animal, wild and bloodthirsty. Children never know if Weasel is real or just a story to scare them.

Eleven-year-old Nathan knows that Weasel exists. In 1839 Nathan and his sister Molly are approached by a strange, mute creature carrying Mama's locket. This locket is a keepsake that Pa carries around his neck. Pa hasn't been home in six days. Maybe this creature could lead Nathan to Pa.

Nathan and Molly follow this odd man named Ezra. Ezra can't talk because Weasel has cut out his tongue.

Maybe Weasel has already captured Pa. What would the cruel Weasel do to Pa?

DeWeese, Gene. **Black Suits from Outer Space.** Dell, 1989. Grades 4-6. First in a series: **The Dandelion Caper** follows.

Science fiction. *Magic; supernatural.*

 Note: This book is similar to the movie Men in Black, although the book was published first. This is recommended for those who think they don't like science fiction.

Calvin Willeford was almost 12 years old when he met his first alien from outer space. At least the first one he knew about. You see, aliens have a special disguise. Aliens wear black suits and a dark hat to fit in with all the many businesspeople working in offices throughout the world. When you look closely, you will see a face without expression, almost like a shadow instead of a face.

Calvin discovers this secret about the Black Suits when his cat finds a ring that's magical. To his surprise, Calvin learns the ring is a signal. The Black Suits approach him for instructions. Calvin's job is to help the aliens cope in this unfamiliar environment. In other words, Calvin is a tourist guide!

Travel on the spaceship with Calvin as he meets the Black Suits from Outer Space.

Dubois, William Pene. **The Twenty-One Balloons.** Scholastic, 1975, 180pp. Grades 5 & Up. First published in 1947. A Newbery Award winner.

Fantasy. *Ecology; magic; science.*

In 1890 there was a big explosion on a Pacific Island called Krakatoa. The sound of the explosion was heard more than 3,000 miles away. That is the greatest distance sound has been known to travel.

Before the explosion, Professor William Waterman Sherman conducted a scientific voyage in a balloon. The Professor learned about multitudes of diamonds on the island of Krakatoa. He also discovered that the inhabitants of the island had several ways of mining and selling the diamonds to their advantage.

Because the inhabitants were living on an island with a volcano, everyone knew it would be only a matter of time before it erupted. Therefore, the Professor and his friends invented the 21 balloons that could carry 80 people off the island to safety.

Will the inhabitants leave the island safely? What happens to the diamonds? This classified information will be revealed between these pages.

Duncan, Lois. **Locked in Time.** Penguin, 1986, 208pp. Grades 5 & Up.

Horror. *Aging; crime; death; magic; occult; supernatural.*

Nore thinks her new stepfamily are the strangest people she has ever met. Those weird vibrations surrounding the Cajun country in Louisiana where they live don't help the eerie atmosphere.

Lisette, her stepmother, is beautiful. Yet she seems threatened by Nore, insisting that Nore has an "awareness of time." What exactly does that mean?

Is Nore's new family caught in some sort of time warp? Are these people locked in time?

Feiffer, Jules. The Man in the Ceiling. Illustrated by the author. HarperCollins, 1993, 185pp. Grades 5 & Up.

Realistic fiction. *Hobbies; peer pressure; self-identity.*

Mini-Man is a super hero with a hood and a cape. Mini-Man is so small that no criminal can catch him, and so no crime will go unpunished.

Mini-Man is a character who Jimmy invented for his own comic book. Jimmy draws Mini-Man so small and useless in appearance that all villains think they can kill him easily, but no one can defeat Mini-Man!

Well, maybe Jimmy's friend Charley Beemer can defeat Mini-Man. Charley is the only person outside Jimmy's family who is allowed to see his drawings. Charley thinks Mini-Man is "boring." He wants Jimmy to draw a character called Bullethead whose head is a bullet that can drill through people. Charley wants blood, guts, and severed body parts.

Jimmy knows he should draw Charley's character because it's a "good career move." Drawing comics is Jimmy's way to be popular.

How can Jimmy draw blood and guts when horror makes him sick? Is Jimmy doomed to be a flop as a cartoonist?

Fitzhugh, Louise. Harriet the Spy. Harper, 1964, 294pp. Grades 4-6.

Realistic fiction. *Diaries; ethics; movie novels; peer pressure; responsibility.*

Harriet is a spy. Actually she's a writer, but isn't that the same thing?

Harriet writes down all she sees, hears, and feels. If it isn't nice, so what? A writer can't be nice. That would be boring.

Unfortunately, Harriet has lost her journal. She doesn't care if Marion or Beth Ellen read her journal, but she certainly doesn't want her friends Janie or Sport reading it. It's truthful, but it's also hurtful.

Who has Harriet's journal? Is it the members of the newly formed "Spy Catchers Club"? Just what would the club members do to Harriet once they catch her?

Fleischman, Paul. The Half-a-Moon Inn. Illustrated by Kathy Jacobi. Harper & Row, 1980, 88pp. Grades 4-8.

Folklore. *Abuse; disability (physical); magic; Middle Ages; occult; supernatural.*

Long ago and far away lived a young boy. He had never been away from home or apart from his mother. One day his mother thought Aaron could stay home alone while she went to the fair in Craftsbury. When she didn't return, Aaron left the security of his home to find her.

Oh, yes, one thing I should mention: Aaron is mute. He has not been able to speak since birth. This becomes a problem, for how can he communicate his concern for his mother to strangers? True, he can read and write, but, to his horror, he discovers most people in the Middle Ages can't read!

Aaron is kidnapped by the ugly hag Miss Grackle who owns The Half-a-Moon Inn. She forces him to steal from the visitors to the inn. Aaron despairs of ever returning home until he cleverly devises a plan for his escape.

Fleischman, Sid. **The Whipping Boy.**
Illustrated by Peter Sis. Troll, 1986,
90pp. Grades 4-6.
A Newbery Award winner.

Adventure. *Class conflict; Middle Ages;
orphans; rites of passage; runaway.*

Prince Brat is up to his old tricks again. Bring out the whipping boy!

What's Prince Brat done this time? This time he tied the lords and ladies' powdered wigs to the backs of their oak chairs. Last week he dumped bullfrogs in the moat. The week before he hog-greased the saddles of all the knights.

Of course, no one can beat the Prince, no matter what kind of brat he is. So Jemmy, an orphan boy, has the dubious honor of being the boy who is whipped.

One night Jemmy is awakened by the Prince. The Prince is bored with his life of ease and is going to run away. The Prince needs a servant and so Jemmy has a new job. Of course, Jemmy plans to do some running away himself. The first chance he gets!

Their plans go awry. The boys hadn't planned to be kidnapped by Hold-Your-Nose Billy, the legendary murderer!

Fritz, Jean. **George Washington's
Breakfast.** Illustrated by Paul Galdone.
(Pbk.) Coward-McCann, 1969.
Grades 3-6.

Biography. *American Revolutionary War;
hobbies; politics.*

What did George Washington eat for breakfast?

That's what George Washington Allen wants to know about his namesake and the first President of the United States. He wants to know everything the first President did and said, including what he ate for breakfast.

George Washington Allen goes on a search to find out the answer. He goes to the library; to Washington, D.C.; and even to Mount Vernon to find out what President Washington ate for breakfast.

We get to learn many fascinating facts about the President, too. For instance, George Washington wore size 13 shoes and could bend a horseshoe with his bare hands.

Oh yes, just what did George Washington eat for breakfast? Read this book by Jean Fritz and find out for yourself.

Gantos, Jack. **Head or Tails: Stories
from the Sixth Grade.** Farrar,
Strauss & Giroux, 1994, 151pp. Grades
4-7. A Young Readers' Choice Award
winner. First in a series: **Jack's New
Power: Stories from a Caribbean
Year** and **Jack's Black Book** follow.

Humor. *Diaries; family; school; secrets.*

I'll never be President, just the Vice President. I won't be a gangster godfather, just the stooge killer. I'm a copycat. I never come up with great ideas. I watch someone do it, then I copy it.

Like this diary. My sister Betsy got a diary, so I had to have one. Only problem is that I can't write a word. Not one word. I've been putting in squished spiders and photos and baseball cards, but no secret thoughts.

Yet these things keep happening, like the UFO Hot Line, the hurricane, the alligator that ate my dog, and the day my brother shot down an airplane with his finger.

Hey, maybe I do have something to say after all!

Garland, Sherry. **The Silent Storm**. Harcourt, Brace, 1993, 240pp. Grades 6 & Up.

Realistic fiction. *Death; disability (physical); survival.*

 Note: This book is a favorite for those readers who love disaster movies.

Before the great storm that changed her life, Alyssa loved to hear about hurricanes, typhoons, and cyclones. Instead of fairy tales, Alyssa begged to hear about storms at sea.

One day Alyssa got her wish. A storm hit her home. It was just like the storms in the sailors' tales she had heard and read. One thing she didn't know was that the wind can tear families and people's lives apart, destroying them forever.

Maybe they had told Alyssa. Maybe she just hadn't listened.

George, Jean Craighead. **Julie of the Wolves.** Illustrated by John Schoenherr. Harper & Row, 1972, 170pp. Grades 4-8. A Newbery Award winner. First in a series: **Julie** follows.

Adventure. *Animals (wolves); Native Americans; rites of passage; survival.*

"Amaroq, ilaya, wolf, my friend."

Julie Edwards Miyax Kapugen calls to the wolf in both Eskimo and English, hoping to gain his trust. Eventually the wolf befriends Julie and leads her to food and to his den. Julie becomes friends with all the wolves.

At 13, Julie had no close friends. She ran away from her abusive husband to meet a ship to take her to San Francisco. Her pen pal Amy lived there and was always writing Julie, "When are you coming to visit me?" After seven days and nights of her journey, Julie was tired and hungry. Maybe her new friends could help her face the bitter cold Alaskan winter.

Through the wolves, Julie learned how to survive. Instead of escaping to San Francisco, Julie's journey would lead her home. She would learn to take pride in her heritage and would even locate her missing father. At last Julie was finally coming home.

Giff, Patricia Reilly. **Lily's Crossing.** Delacorte, 1997, 180pp. Grades 5-8. A Newbery Honor book.

Historical fiction. *Friendship; orphans; responsibility; survival; World War II.*

 Note: This book can be a thought-provoking read-aloud and can be enjoyed by middle school students as well.

Lily was a liar. She didn't want to lie, but she had a huge imagination. Once she said her aunt was an important spy against the Nazis. Another time she said her father was in the Secret Service. Lily thought her lies made life interesting.

Lily was also a sneak. She tiptoed to her neighbor's house and heard Albert Orban say he had to find Ruth. Lily was intrigued. Who was Ruth?

Eventually Lily learned that Albert had escaped from Budapest, Hungary. His sister Ruth was still in France. His parents had been killed for opposing the Nazis.

Then Lily told Albert her biggest lie ever. That lie almost cost Albert his life.

Greene, Constance C. **A Girl Called Al.**
Illustrated by Byron Barton. Viking,
1969, 127pp. Grades 4-6. First in a
series: **I Know You, Al; Your Old
Pal, Al; A(Lexandra) the Great;
Just Plain Al**; and **Al's Blind Date**
follow.

Realistic fiction. *Death; friendship; illness
(physical); women's issues.*

A girl called Al just moved in down the hall. Al is short for Alexandra, which she hates. Al hates many things, but especially she hates conformists.

"What's a conformist?" I ask.

"A conformist follows the crowd. I'm a nonconformist. That means I don't follow the crowd. I'm different," she explains.

She is, too. A nonconformist. And different. Like, she wants to take Shop instead of Cooking and Sewing. Also, she is practically the only girl in the entire school with pigtails.

Did I mention she's my best friend? Well, she is, along with Mr. Richards, the custodian of our apartment building.

Mr. Richards taught Al and me how to polish his kitchen floor by strapping rags to our shoes and skating on his floor. Isn't that neat? We three were like The Three Musketeers. Except when Mr. Richards got sick. That was a shock to Al and me.

Join us in our adventures in the *Al* series.

Grove, Vicki. **Rimwalkers.** G. P.
Putman's Sons, 1993, 221pp.
Grades 5 & Up.

Horror. *Disability (physical); occult;
supernatural; survival.*

Look out for the rimwalkers!

My cousins Rennie and Elijah, my younger sister Sara, and I are rimwalkers. We like *rimwalking*, that is, walking on the edge of a rail or board usually high above the ground.

Who is that ghostly young boy waving in the attic window of a deserted house? Grandfather says he's a mirage, something we thought we saw, but didn't. Gram says it is the ghost of Americus, our great-great uncle who was drowned many years ago. We just have to find out. The only way is by rimwalking.

One day a tragedy occurs that will change the rimwalkers forever.

Hahn, Mary Downing. **The Time of
the Witch.** Clarion Books, 1982,
171pp. Grades 6-8.

Realistic fiction. *Crime; divorce; problem
parents; revenge; stepparents.*

"Don't get mad, get even."

Laura's parents are getting a divorce. That's why Laura wears her T-shirt of revenge. Laura is trying to think of a way to get even with her parents for even thinking about divorcing. She is especially mad at her dad for considering marrying someone else.

When the old woman Maude admires Laura's T-shirt, Laura becomes friends with the eccentric woman. Laura has heard that Maude is a witch and asks Maude for help in getting her parents back together.

What Laura doesn't know is that Maude has a very good reason for getting even!

Hahn, Mary Downing. **Wait till Helen Comes.** Clarion Books, 1986, 184pp. Grades 5 & Up.
A Young Readers' Choice Award winner.

Horror. *Occult; revenge; rivalry; stepparents; supernatural.*

"Look, Heather, it's a graveyard," I whispered to my seven-year-old stepsister.

We were taking a walk near the property my mom and stepfather bought. We were exploring the area behind the church Mom and Dave were planning to renovate into House Beautiful.

How weird to own property where dead people are buried! How will I be able to sleep at night?

What's even weirder is the grave Heather discovers. The tombstone is inscribed "H. E. H." with Heather's initials! The grave is of a seven-year-old girl just like Heather. It turns out she died in a fire just like Heather's mom.

One day I spot Heather talking to the grave. "Oh, Helen. Will you be my friend? I'll do anything you say if you'll be my friend."

Do you believe in ghosts? Better wait till Helen comes, then tell me your decision.

Hamilton, Virginia. **The House of Dies Drear.** Illustrated by Eros Keith. Macmillan, 1968, 246pp. Grades 6 & Up. First in a series: **The Mystery of Dies Drear** follows.

Horror. *African Americans; Civil War; interracial relations; racism; runaways.*

 Note: This book also contains information about the Underground Railroad.

Beware of the house of Dies Drear. Beware of the house that once harbored runaway slaves during the Civil War. Beware of the house that carries a century-old legend of two fugitive slaves killed while trying to escape this house. Beware of the ghost that haunts the house of Dies Drear.

The Small family buy the Drear House because it is a historic site of the Underground Railroad. Is the house haunted like people say? Strange things do happen; strange people do appear and disappear like ghosts. What do those Greek crosses mean? Are the crosses a warning to leave?

You won't leave your seat as you take a tour of *The House of Dies Drear.*

Henry, Marguerite. **Misty of Chincoteague.** Illustrated by Wesley Dennis. Rand McNally, 1947, 158pp. Grades 4-6. First in a series: **Sea Star** and **Stormy, Misty's Foal** follow.

Adventure. *Animals (horses); responsibility.*

"You'll never catch Phantom. That wild horse is a piece of sky and wind. She's never been caught in all her years on Assateague Island," Grandpa warned Maureen and Paul.

Paul and Maureen knew Phantom would be difficult to capture, but they worked on a plan that might work. What they hadn't counted on was also capturing a beautiful brand-new, silvery-gray colt!

"I'll call her Misty," Paul whispered.

Houston, James. **Frozen Fire: A Tale of Courage.** Illustrated by the author. Atheneum, 1977, 149pp. Grades 4 & Up. First in a series: **Black Diamonds: A Search for Arctic Treasure** follows.

Adventure. *Native Americans; problem parents; rites of passage; survival.*

Fasten your seat belt. You're on a high impact adventure of survival in the Canadian Arctic. Join 13-year-old Matthew Morgan and his Eskimo friend, Kayak, as they battle wind storms, starvation, and wild animals during their search for Matthew's father.

Matthew's father is a geologist dreaming of discovering gold or copper on one of his excursions. One day Matthew's father and his pilot friend, Charlie, don't return home.

Matthew and Kayak borrow a snowmobile to bring back the lost pair. Instead they run out of fuel and run into danger of starvation and frostbite, not to mention the hungry polar bears and wolves!

Based on a true story, *Frozen Fire* will freeze you into your seat for a chilling adventure.

Howe, James & Deborah. **Bunnicula: A Rabbit-Tale of Mystery.** Illustrated by Alan Daniel. Atheneum, 1979. Grades 3-5. A Young Readers' Choice Award. Part of a series by James Howe: **Howliday Inn, The Celery Stalks at Midnight, Nighty-Nightmare,** and **Return to Howliday Inn** follow.

Humor. *Animals; occult; supernatural.*

My name is Harold, and I am a dog. I live with the Monroes. Also residing with me is a cat, Chester. Chester has been reading since he's been a kitten, so he has quite an imagination.

Anyway, Chester thinks our new pet rabbit is a vampire. If you ask me, I think Chester has been reading one too many horror thrillers.

Join us on our hilarious adventures in *Bunnicula: A Rabbit-Tale of Mystery.*

Hurwitz, Johanna. **Baseball Fever.** Illustrated by Ray Cruz. Dell, 1981, 128pp. Grades 4-6.

Sports. *Hobbies; men's issues; problem parents; sports (baseball).*

Ezra has baseball fever. His favorite month is April, when the baseball season opens.

Ezra's father hates April because taxes are due to the IRS. He also hates baseball because he doesn't understand it. He's from Germany and a professor, so it doesn't make sense to him. He thinks an "RBI" is "rubbish brought in"! Professor Feldman wants Ezra to forget baseball and to play chess instead.

How can Ezra infect his dad with baseball fever?

Hurwitz, Johanna. **Much Ado About Aldo.** Morrow, 1978, 95pp. Grades 4-6. Part of a series, including: **Aldo Applesauce; Aldo Ice Cream;** and **Aldo Peanut Butter.**

Humor. *Animals; ethics; responsibility; school; science.*

Note: This is a popular series with those who enjoy Judy Blume's Fudge series (see page 11).

Aldo Sossi is the most interested student in Mrs. Dowling's third grade. Not interesting, *interested.* Everything fascinates Aldo.

Aldo is interested in why "one" was spelled that way. He enjoys the multiplication tables in Mathematics. In Social Studies he is never bored with the filmstrips about life in other countries.

Aldo loves Science most of all. For an experiment, some chameleons are put into a same tank with some crickets. Now Aldo has a cause. He is interested in saving the crickets. He has to take drastic action–even if he's sent to the principal's office!

James, Mary. **Shoebag.** (Pbk.) Scholastic, 1990, 125pp. Grades 4-6.

Humor. *School; secrets; self-identity.*

Note: Under the pen name M. E. Kerr, Mary James is a well-known young adult author of realistic fiction.

I am Shoebag. I was named after my place of birth. My mother is named Drainboard. My father is named Under the Toaster.

Recently I have changed into an ugly, hideous creature. I am no longer small with antennae. I no longer have two back legs, two middle legs, and two front legs. I believe I am now one of those horrible things called humans.

How did this happen? How can I go back to what I was? How can I go back to being a cockroach?

Johnson, Angela. **Toning the Sweep.** Orchard Books, 1993, 103 pp. Grades 5 & Up. The 1994 Coretta Scott King Award winner.

Realistic fiction. *African Americans; death; illness (physical).*

Note: This is a short book that discusses complex issues. I recommend this one as a read-aloud and for middle school students, too.

Ola has cancer.

Ola's granddaughter Emily and her daughter Diane are "toning the sweep." Way down south in South Carolina, when someone dies a relative gets a hammer and hits a sweep, a kind of plow, to let everyone know about the death. That ringing sound sends a person's soul straight to heaven. It's always better to know when someone's dying so folks can prepare to tone the sweep.

Emily and Diane are toning the sweep in the only way they know. They're preparing a videotape on memories of Ola. That way they'll always keep Ola close to their hearts.

King-Smit, Dick. **Three Terrible Trins.** Illustrated by Mark Teague. Crown, 1994, 105pp. Grades 3-5.

Fantasy. *Animals (mice); class conflict; love; survival.*

This is the story of the terrible trins–Thomas, Richard, and Henry Gray. Trins are triplets and the Grays are mice.

Mrs. Gray is an Attic mouse of good birth. She is descended from a clan of mice who considered themselves superior to the Cellarmice. After being widowed three times, she promises herself that her trins will be guerrilla fighters in the cause of mousedom.

The Terrible Trins take great delight in taunting the cats on Orchard Farms. They even befriend a Cellarmouse named Kevin Coaldust to help them with their mission.

Kevin Coaldust has fallen in love with Mrs. Gray. Can a Cellarmouse find happiness with a well-bred lady from the Attic?

Klause, Annette Curtis. **Alien Secrets.** Delacorte, 1993, 227pp. Grades 5-7.

Science fiction. *End-of-the-world; revenge; supernatural; war.*

 Note. Even students who think they don't like science fiction will enjoy this one.

Ghosts and aliens on a spaceship? What's going on? Lots of mystery, drama, and adventure, that's what.

Puck is on a spaceship to visit her parents who are doing research on the planet Shoon. Puck meets the alien Hush, who is returning to his home planet Shoon in disgrace. Hush was given a symbol of freedom for his people and the treasure has been stolen. Puck and Hush know the treasure is on the spaceship. If they find it, they will free the ghosts that haunt the ship.

Try this science fiction adventure. It's out of this world!

Konigsburg, E. L. **From the Mixed-Up Files of Mrs. Basil E. Frankweiler.** Illustrated by the author. Antheneum, 1987, 159pp. Grades 4-6. A Newbery Award winner.

Realistic fiction. *Movie novels; responsibility; runaways.*

Claudia had it all planned perfectly. She would run away from home with her younger brother, Jamie. Claudia wanted to run away to a safe, warm place like the Metropolitan Museum in New York City. She discovered a discarded train pass. She regarded that as an invitation. They would leave on Wednesday. They would pack their clothes in their musical instrument cases. Once they arrived in the museum, they would enter as any tourists, but they wouldn't leave. Yes, Claudia had planned it perfectly.

Once Jamie was almost caught. He saw a janitor when the museum was closed. "Where did you come from?" asked the startled janitor. "My mother says I came from heaven," Jamie said as he walked out of the bathroom.

How do I know all this? I'm Mrs. Basil E. Frankweiler. You'll have to read the book to learn how I come into this mystery about a statue within the museum.

Konigsburg, E. L. **Jennifer, Hecate, Macbeth, William McKinley and Me, Elizabeth.** Dell, 1967, 117pp. Grades 4-6.

Realistic fiction. *African Americans; friendship; interracial relations; magic; supernatural.*

 Note: This booktalk appears more sinister than the book really is. Jennifer has an active imagination that requires her to invent games to make a friend.

I met my best and only friend, Jennifer, on Halloween. She was sitting high in a tree, so I saw her feet first. Her Pilgrim shoes were dangling from her feet, so I said, "You're gonna lose your shoes."

"Witches never lose anything," she said.

"But you're a Pilgrim for Halloween," I replied.

"This is a disguise. I'm really a witch disguised as a Pilgrim," Jennifer explained.

That's how we met. Jennifer promised to teach me how to be a witch. Every Saturday morning she would give me instructions like eating a raw egg or drinking black coffee for a week. We would sit in our magic circle and talk about everything. We even had a toad, called Hilary Ezra.

We had our first fight over Hilary Ezra. Jennifer wanted me to put the toad in boiling water for one of her spells. Or did she? Why did she hesitate so long?

Who is Jennifer? Is she a witch or just a girl who needs a friend?

Konigsburg, E. L. **The View from Saturday.** Atheneum Books for Young Readers, 1996. Grades 5 & Up. A Newbery Award winner.

Realistic fiction. *African Americans; Asian Americans; disability (physical); interracial relations; school.*

 **Note:** This book sympathetically portrays a teacher who is a paraplegic. This is recommended as a read-aloud.

When Mrs. Eva Marie Olinsky was asked how she selected her team for the Academic Bowl, she always gave different answers. When she was being humorous, she said she chose a brunette, a red-head, a blond, and a student with hair as black as newsprint. Another time she said the team became a team when they called themselves The Souls.

The truth is that Mrs. Olinsky didn't know how she chose her team of sixth graders. It hardly matters now. The Souls had beaten the seventh and eighth graders. Now they were headed to Albany, New York, to compete for the state trophy.

Just what makes this team called The Souls so special?

L'Engle, Madeleine. **A Wrinkle in Time.** Bantam Doubleday Dell, 1962, 190pp. Grades 4-7. A Newbery Award winner. First in a series: **A Wind in the Door** and **A Swiftly Tilting Planet** follow.

Science fiction. *Magic; revenge; supernatural; survival; time travel.*

"By the way, there is such a thing as a tesseract," Mrs. Whatsit nods to Mrs. Murry. Like a puff of smoke, Mrs. Whatsit disappears as quickly as she arrived.

"Mother! What's wrong?" Meg asks her trembling mother.

"The tesseract–" Mrs. Murry whispers. "How did she know? Only a few people know about the scientific concept of a wrinkle in time. Maybe she can help us find your missing father."

Mrs. Murry's hunch is correct. Mrs. Whatsit and her friends Mrs. Who and Mrs. Which know where Mr. Murry is. The three guardian spirits take Meg, her brother Charles Wallace, and their friend Calvin to the planet Camazotz. This planet is controlled by IT, an evil force. IT immediately hypnotizes Charles Wallace and forces him to agree with IT.

Now IT has both Mr. Murry and Charles Wallace under its control. How can they escape?

Levitin, Sonia. **The Golem and the Dragon Girl.** Dial, 1993, 187pp. Grades 6 & Up.

Horror. *Asian Americans; interracial relations; Jews; occult; stepparents; supernatural.*

Is the house really haunted? Is there a golem haunting the house? In case you don't know, a *golem* is a ghost that grows big enough to eventually kill a person.

Jonathan thinks he invented the golem with his negative thoughts about his stepfather, Steve. It was Steve and Jonathan's mother who decided to move into the new house. The house used to be owned by the Wangs.

Laurel Wang thinks the ghost is the dragon spirit of her great-grandfather. She believes that a dragon captures all a person's fears into one spirit. That dragon is still in that house that her family left. Laurel thinks she must be the one to release the dragon.

Together Laurel and Jonathan try to destroy the ghost. Golem, ghost, or dragon, this book by Sonia Levitin will haunt you.

Lowry, Lois. **Number the Stars.** Houghton Mifflin, 1989, 137pp.; (Pbk.) Dell, 1992. Grades 4 & Up. A Newbery Award winner.

Historical fiction. *Europe (Denmark); Holocaust; Jews; religious prejudice; World War II.*

"How brave are you, little Annemarie?" Uncle Henrik asked his 10-year-old niece.

Annemarie couldn't answer that question because she had never needed courage. Later Annemarie learned how much courage was required to survive the brutality of the Nazis in her occupied country of Denmark. Annemarie's bravery was tested when she tried to save her Jewish friend, Ellen Rosen, from the Nazis. Annemarie learned that courage comes with convictions.

This Newbery Award-winning book is based on the true story of the Danish people. The Danes saved almost 7,000 Jews during World War II. They secretly sent Jews to Sweden on fishing boats. No other country took such a strong stand against the Nazis. The Danes are proof that people can make a difference against tyranny.

Lunn, Janet. **The Root Cellar.** Puffin Books, 1981, 229pp. Grades 5 & Up.

Fantasy. *Civil War; rites of passage; time travel.*

The root cellar looked like any ordinary, underground cellar. It was the kind of place you might store canned goods and winter vegetables. One day, 12-year-old Rose ran down the stairs to the dark cellar. When she climbed the steps, she was in another place and time. She was back in time more than 100 years ago.

Right away Rose became friends with Susan and Will. Of course, her new friends ignored Rose when she said she came from another time. Susan and Will liked Rose, even if she did say strange things. Rose was able to go back in time again and again. All she had to do is go to the root cellar.

One day Susan needed Rose's help. Will had enlisted in the Union army during the War Between the States. He hadn't contacted Susan in three years. Susan and Rose must go to the Civil War battlefields to find Will.

Will Rose and Susan rescue Will? Will Rose ever escape back to the future?

MacLachlan, Patricia. **Baby.** Delacorte, 1993, 132pp. Grades 4 & Up.

Realistic fiction. *Adoption; ethics; responsibility.*

"This is Sophie. She is almost a year old and she is good. I love her. I will come back for her someday."

This note was pinned to the baby in the basket. The Baldelli family immediately took Sophie into their home and their hearts, but they always knew the mother would be back for Sophie.

How do you give a baby all your love and know that one day you will also have to give her away? Perhaps Grandma Byrd put it best when she said: "We are giving Sophie something to take away with her when she goes."

"What?" asked Lalo.

"Us," Grandma said firmly.

You will also take away warm memories when you leave the final chapter of *Baby* by Patricia MacLachlan.

MacLachlan, Patricia. **Sarah, Plain and Tall.** HarperTrophy, 1985, 58pp. Grades 3-5. A Newbery Award winner. First in a series: **Skylark** follows.

Historical fiction. *Movie novels; pioneer life; stepparents.*

"I've placed an advertisement in the newspapers. For help."

"You mean a housekeeper?" I asked.

"No," said Papa slowly. "Not a housewife. A wife."

My brother Caleb and I stared at Papa. Mama died when Caleb was born. Our neighbor, Matthew, had written for a wife, and Maggie from Tennessee finally arrived. But for Papa to do the same!

Papa reached into his pocket. "I have received a letter from Sarah Elizabeth Wheaton who lives in Maine."

We began corresponding with Sarah who loves the sea and owns a cat.

We wait and wonder. Will Sarah be nice? Will she like us? Will she stay?

Mahy, Margaret. **The Pirates'
Mixed-Up Voyage.** Illustrated by
Margaret Chamberlain. Dial Books for
Young Readers, 1993, 180pp.
Grades 4-7.

Humor. *Crime; magic.*

Let me introduce you to Lionel Wafer, manager of the "Ye Olde
Pyratte Shippe Tea Shoppe." Meet Toothpick, a parrot who screams
"Doom and Destiny!" to customers. Get to know Toad, the cook with
tin ears, and the waiter named Brace-and-Bit.

These characters have two dreams: to become pirates and to
become rich. Is that unreasonable in these troubled times?

They set sail on *The Sinful Sausage* as pirates. To get money
they must kidnap millionaire Humbert Cash-Cash. They just can't
seem to find him on the Thousands of Islands.

Know why they can't find Humbert Cash-Cash? None of the
pirates can read! That's very hard when the pirates need to understand a map.

Climb aboard *The Sinful Sausage* to join these hilarious characters on *The Pirates' Mixed-up Voyage.*

Martin, Ann M. **Ma and Pa Dracula.**
(Pbk.) Scholastic Trade, 1991, 122pp.
Grades 4-6.

Humor. *Occult; secrets; self-identity;
supernatural.*

Jonathan Primave is old enough to notice some unusual things
about his parents. For one thing, they look different from anyone
else. The have two fang-like top teeth, long fingernails like claws, and
pointed ears. They sleep in coffins all day and work in a blood bank
at night. If Jonathan asks them how old they are, they never give a
straight answer. Once Ma said, "As old as the hills." Pa said, "212." Is
that a joke or what?

Jonathan asks his parents for the truth. He gets the shock of
his life. He is adopted. His parents are really vampires. That's why
Jonathan has never been to school.

Now Jonathan wants a normal life. He wants to go to school
and to make friends. He wants to give a Halloween party for all his
new friends. Here's the problem: Will his friends be a trick or a
treat?

Medaris, Angela Shelf. **Dare to Dream: Coretta Scott King and the Civil Rights Movement.** Illustrated by Anna Rich. Lodestar Books, 1994, 60pp. Grades 4-6.

Biography. *African Americans; interracial relations; love; racism; responsibility.*

Do you remember Martin Luther King gave a speech, "I have a dream"?

His wife, Coretta Scott King, had a dream, also. When she was young, her dream was to be an opera singer. As she grew older, she changed her dream to a peaceful future for all races. Her husband wanted the same. Coretta Scott King has devoted her life to keep their dream alive.

When we dare to dream and put our dreams to action, we can change society. They certainly did. Before the 1960's Civil Rights movement, African Americans lived separately from whites. In public they had different bathrooms and even separate drinking fountains labeled "Colored."

Many changes have taken place since then, thanks to the actions of some brave people. Read about Coretta Scott King's inspirational life. Maybe you too can find the courage to dare to dream.

Naidoo, Beverly. **Journey to Jo'burg.** (Pbk.) Illustrated by Eric Velasques. HarperTrophy, 1986, 75pp. Grades 5 & Up. First in a series: **Chain of Fire** follows.

Historical fiction. *Apartheid; interracial relations; racism; single parents; South Africa.*

Note: *Students may need to know about apartheid, a legal form of racial segregation in South Africa from 1948 to 1991. This is also an excellent choice for middle school students.*

My brother Tiro and I began a long journey from our small village to Johannesburg, South Africa. Our baby sister was sick. We had to tell our Mma, who works in Jo'burg.

We don't understand why Mma couldn't live with us at home. She said she had to work to feed us and that we were not allowed in the white people's area. I learned about the South African government and how our color kept us from separate from white people. It was called *apartheid*. By law, all races of people were separated.

How strange. If my sister hadn't been so ill, we would not have come to Jo'burg. On this journey I discovered so much about my family, my country, and myself.

Travel with us on this journey to Jo'burg.

Norton, Mary. **The Borrowers.**
Illustrated by Beth & Joe Krush.
Harcourt, Brace, 1981. First published
in 1952. Grades 4 & Up. First in a
series: **The Borrowers Afield; The
Borrowers Afloat; The
Borrowers Aloft;** and **The
Borrowers Avenged** follow.

Fantasy. *Magic; secrets; survival.*

Where are safety pins and needles when you need them? They disappear. What about pencils, thimbles, and matchboxes? Always gone when you need them.

Let me tell you where all those items have gone. The Borrowers have them. The Borrowers are tiny people who borrow human objects. They never return them, of course. They need these safety pins, needles, and pencils to survive.

Under a clock in a large house live Homily, Pod, and Arrietty Clock. Arrietty is bored waiting for her father Pod. All Arrietty does is write in her diary. What good is it to have a diary when there's nothing to write?

One day Pod arrives, shaking and trembling. "We must leave. I've been spotted. By a boy, of all things!"

Arrietty's heart ticks like the clock where they live. At last something exciting has happened. She knows the boy will change her life from a dull routine to an exciting adventure!

O'Brien, Robert C. **Mrs. Frisby and
the Rats of NIMH.** Illustrated by
Zena Bernstein. Aladdin, 1971, 233pp.
Grades 5-7. A Newbery Award and
Lewis Carroll Shelf Award winner; an
ALA Notable Book. Series continued by
Jane Leslie Conly: **Rasco and the
Rats of NIMH** and **R-T,
Margaret, and the Rats of
NIMH** follow.

Fantasy. *Animals (rats); revenge;
rivalry; runaways; science; survival.*

"Stop where you are," said the rat. "No field mouse is allowed inside."

"I'm Mrs. Frisby. I was told by the owl to see the Rats of NIMH to save my son Timothy. You see, we must move soon and Timothy is so sick . . ."

"Mrs. Frisby? Any relation to Jonathan Frisby?"

"Yes, sir. He was my husband before he was killed by Dragon the cat."

"Madam, it is an honor to meet you. Come in. We'll see what we can do."

Mrs. Frisby had never seen anything like it. Electricity! Carpeted floors! Stained glass windows! An elevator! She saw dozens of rats, standing, talking, carrying papers, scurrying.

Mrs. Frisby learned that these intelligent rats had escaped from the National Institute of Mental Health. The rats had grown bigger and more intelligent due to injections by scientists. Because scientists taught the rats how to read, they unknowingly taught rats how to run away. Later the rats designed their own advanced colony.

Mrs. Frisby breathed a sigh of relief. She was certain the Rats of NIMH could help her family.

Orlev, Uri. Lydia, Queen of Palestine. English translation by Hillel Halkin. Houghton Mifflin, 1993, 170pp. Grades 5 & Up.

Historical fiction. *Jews; Middle East; problem parents; religious prejudice; revenge; World War II.*

I admit it. I am a terror. For one thing, I believe I am a princess. I am going to marry Prince Michael, son of the King of Rumania. Then we would move to Palestine and live happily ever after.

Why don't you find out if my fantasy comes true?

Paterson, Katherine. Flip-Flop Girl. Lodestar, 1994, 120pp. Grades 4-8.

Realistic fiction. *African Americans; ethics; interracial relations; problem parents; responsibility.*

Lupe is the flip-flop girl. She always wears bright orange flip-flops instead of the usual sneakers. Lupe is always in trouble at school. She is always doing strange things, like naming a pumpkin after her father. He is in prison for murdering her mother.

This time the flip-flop girl is innocent. Lupe did not carve her initials on her teacher's car. How does Vinnie Matthews know this? Vinnie knows Lupe is innocent because Vinnie carved the initials herself.

Why is the flip-flop girl willing to take all the blame for something she knows she didn't do?

Paulsen, Gary. Puppies, Dogs and Blue Northers: Reflections on Being Raised by a Pack of Sled Dogs. Illustrated by Ruth Wright Paulsen. Scholastic, 1996, 80pp. Grades 4-7.

Nonfiction. *Animals (dogs); death; responsibility; trust.*

Dogs live in sounds, always in noise. They make sad songs and happy songs. Sometime dogs harmonize. Sometimes dogs (especially puppies) sing off-key. People come to know their own dog's sounds as parents know the cries of their babies.

I know all my dogs' sounds and habits, especially Cookie's. Cookie was my primary sled dog for close to 14,000 miles. She ran one full Iditarod. She even saved my life a time or two.

I'm Gary Paulsen, the author of many adventure books, like *Hatchet*. However, this story is true. Join me on a journey with my favorite sled dog, Cookie.

Paulsen, Gary. Tracker. Simon & Schuster for Young People, 1984, 90pp. Grades 5-7.

Realistic fiction. *Illness (cancer); men's issues; responsibility; rites of passage; sports (hunting).*

Note: This book is similar in theme and style to the book **Wringer,** by Jerry Spinelli.

"This year you will go hunting alone, " said John's grandfather. "I'll stay home and do the chores."

John knew why his grandfather wasn't going on their deer hunt this year. John's grandfather was dying of cancer. This year would be difficult without his grandfather, but John planned to do his best.

In the past John had killed many deer. After killing his first deer, he was sad, but that feeling passed quickly. Then it wasn't difficult to kill anymore. After all, they ate the meat all winter long.

This time, without his grandfather, John began the hunt. He spotted a doe that was perfect. He followed her for two days. He almost had her a couple of times, but she escaped. The third time he spotted the doe, he raised his rifle and tightened the trigger.

Why was he hesitating?

Pearce, Philippa. **Tom's Midnight Garden.** Lippincott, 1964, 229 pp. Grades 5 & Up. A Carnegie Medal winner.

Fantasy. *Aging; magic; rites of passage; time travel.*

Magic begins when the grandfather clock strikes 13. Tom is transported back in time to a mystical garden. In the midnight garden he meets Hetty, a child of the past.

Tom's life is much more exciting in the midnight garden. During the day Tom is recovering from an illness in a boarding house with old people. I mean, Tom likes his aunt, his uncle, and Mrs. Bartholomew, the landlady. Yet they aren't young and fun like his magical friend Hetty.

One day the midnight garden disappears. Of course, Hetty disappears, too. Tom is upset until he learns just who Hetty really is.

Now Tom understands the magic of his midnight garden.

Reaver, Chap. **Bill.** Bantam Doubleday Dell Books for Young Readers, 1994, 216pp. Grades 5-7.

Realistic fiction. *Animals (dogs); class conflict; crime; substance abuse (alcohol).*

Me and my dog Bill live alone since Wrong Man put Dad in jail for selling moonshine. Wrong Man is Officer Dudley. He's called Wrong Man because he jailed a mountaineer for selling whiskey to the Wrong Man.

Wrong Man is married to his First Wife, Nell. He calls her First Wife as a joke.

Me, I'm Jessica Gates, known as Jess.

Anyway, I find me a treasure box of coins, and that's when the trouble begins. It almost cost Bill his life. No treasure box is worth to me what Bill is. No sir.

Robinson, Barbara. **The Best School Year Ever.** HarperCollins, 1994, 117pp. Grades 4-6. Second in a series: **The Best Christmas Pageant Ever** precedes.

Humor. *Ethics; school.*

The Herdmans are the meanest kids in our school. Correction: The Herdmans are the meanest kids in the history of the world.

Just how mean are the six Herdman kids? The Herdmans are so mean they aren't allowed in our town hall since Gladys and Ollie put frogs in the drinking fountain.

The Herdmans are so mean they aren't allowed in the post office. Someone actually put all their school pictures right next to the "wanted" posters. Nobody noticed until Ollie Herdman asked the postmaster how much money he could get for his brother Claude.

The Herdman's aren't allowed in the drugstore, movie theater, the A & P, or the Tasti-Lunch Diner.

The only place the Herdmans are allowed is in school. Of course, that's just where the trouble begins!

Rockwell, Thomas. **How to Eat Fried Worms.** Illustrated by Emily McCully. Bantam Doubleday Dell, 1973, 116pp. Grades 4 & Up.

Humor. *Peer pressure; rivalry.*

"Billy, I'll bet you 50 dollars you won't eat 15 worms. I have the money in my savings account."

"Okay, Joe, but I won't eat those green worms that get on tomatoes. And I won't eat them all at once. Instead I'll eat one worm a day for 15 days."

That bet became a major event. Would Billy eat a worm found in manure? How much ketchup and horseradish does it take to smother the taste? Does Billy have to use a knife and fork?

Even Billy's family gets involved. Should they call Poison Control? Should they help Billy fry the worms? Maybe Billy's mom can make a worm casserole!

How do you eat fried worms? With your eyes shut!

Rylant, Cynthia. **The Van Gogh Cafe.** Harcourt, Brace, 1995. Grades 4 & Up.

Fantasy. *Magic.*

Magic is in the Van Gogh Cafe in Flowers, Kansas. Soon word spreads that there is a cafe that is wonderful, like a dream, like a mystery. They say you ought to go there because you will never forget it.

Magic is in the food that cooks itself while Marc writes poetry. It is only when the lemon meringue pies appear that anyone notices the magic. Then more and more magical things happen.

Magic is in the arrival of the famous silent-screen star. Magic is in the arrival of the birds that come to claim some of the legend of the cafe. Magic is in the writer who gains inspiration from just walking into cafe.

Magic may appear to the reader, too. Participate in the enchanting world of *The Van Gogh Cafe.*

Sachar, Louis. **Sideways Stories from Wayside School.** Random, 1985, 128pp. Grades 4-6. First in a series: **Wayside School is Falling Down; Sideways Arithmetic from Wayside School;** and **Wayside School Gets a Little Stranger** follow.

Humor. *Friendship; school.*

Note: This is an excellent read-aloud, chapter by chapter.

The craziest things happen at Wayside School.

Wayside School is all mixed-up because it was supposed to be built with 30 classrooms all next to each other. Instead, the classrooms were built on top of each other like a high-rise apartment.

On the 30th floor are 30 students. Of course, there are 30 unforgettable stories. For example, Nancy is a boy who hates his name. Mac is a girl who hates her name. So they switch names. Now all the students want to switch names. Talk about confusion!

Strange and funny events happen at Wayside. Get enrolled for lots of laughs.

Sachar, Louis. There's a Boy in the Girl's Bathroom. Alfred A. Knopf, 1987, 195pp. Grades 4-7. A Young Readers' Choice Award winner.

Humor. *Friendship; peer pressure; responsibility; self-identity.*

Once it got around the school that a boy was discovered in the girl's bathroom, everyone knew it had to be Bradley Chalkers. Bradley Chalkers was the oldest and toughest guy in school. No one liked Bradley, and that was fine with Bradley. He was proud of his bad reputation, and just as proud he had no friends.

Except for one thing: Bradley Chalkers did not run into the girl's bathroom. It was the new kid in school. This new kid was even meaner and tougher than Bradley. For the first time, Bradley was interested in someone besides himself.

Who was this kid who had the nerve to do something Bradley could never do–run into the girl's bathroom?

San Souci, Robert D. The Faithful Friend. Illustrated by Brian Pinkney. Simon & Schuster for Younger Readers, 1995, unnumbered pages. Grades 4-7.

Folklore. *Caribbean and Latin America; friendship; magic; occult; supernatural; survival.*

> **Note:** This picture story is a recommended read-aloud, especially during Halloween.

Join me on a dangerous journey to the island of Martinique in the Caribbean Sea. This perilous journey is beset by zombies, ghosts, and curses. Distant West Indian drums vibrate throughout the dark night.

Two friends set out on the journey: one to escape with a beautiful girl he plans to marry; the other to help his friend escape the deadly forces plotting to kill the couple.

This faithful friend must decide if he will choose his friend's safety over his own. Because if the faithful friend tells the plans of revenge, he will turn to stone!

Will he remain the faithful friend?

Snyder, Zilpha Keatley. The Egypt Game. Antheneum, 1967, 215pp. Grades 4-7.

Mysteries/thrillers. *African Americans; Asian Americans; crime; friendship; hobbies; interracial relations.*

Want to play the Egypt Game?

April Hall and Melanie Ross love imagining that they are living in ancient Egypt. Together they invent the Egypt Game. They use a lean-to shed as their temple. They invent rites and ceremonies for the gods. They use a black rock as a magical stone.

They even allow new members to join. Of course, they are required to be creative and imaginative. Melanie's younger brother, Marshall, becomes a Pharaoh. Later, Elizabeth, Ken, and Toby join the Egypt Game and add their own creative style to the rituals.

Everything is going fine until the murder of a young child occurs in the neighborhood. Police say the murderer is probably someone living in the neighborhood.

Are the members of the Egypt Game in grave danger? As one mummy said to the other, "My lips are sealed!"

Speare, Elizabeth George. **The Witch of Blackbird Pond.** Bantam Doubleday Dell, 1986, 223pp. First published in 1958. Grades 5 & Up. A Newbery Award winner.

Historical fiction. *Ethics; immigrants; religious prejudice; women's issues.*

 Older students love this book as well.

"There's Connecticut Colony," said the captain's son, Nat Eaton. "How does it look?"

Standing on the deck of the ship, Kit Tyler was disappointed in the bleak horizon. She was accustomed to the sunshine of Barbados, a Caribbean island. She would find the new land's strict, Puritan ways cold and forbidding. However, Kit had no choice. Orphaned and homeless, she was sent to live with her Uncle Matthew, her Aunt Rachel, and her cousins, Judith and Mercy.

Kit had a hard adjustment. In 1687 most Puritan girls weren't supposed to read, swim, or wear bright clothing. Kit did all of these things. She was independent, too. For instance, she liked to visit Hannah, an old Quaker woman known as the Witch of Blackbird Pond. She also enjoyed spending time with Nat. Both of her new friends were forbidden to her, but Kit disobeyed her uncle's orders.

When Kit's friendship with Hannah is discovered, Kit must face the wrath and suspicions of the village. To her horror, Kit is accused of witchcraft!

Spinelli, Jerry. **Crash.** Alfred Knopf, 1996, 162pp. Grades 5 & Up.

Realistic fiction. *Friendship; peer pressure; religious prejudice.*

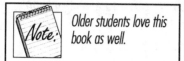 Jerry Spinelli's novels can also be introduced and enjoyed in the middle school. His humor usually covers a poignant issue.

My real name is John. John Coogan. Everybody calls me Crash, even my parents. See, when I was little, I crashed into my cousin with my football helmet. As far as I can tell, I've always been crashing–into people, into things, with or without a football helmet.

Wait. I lied. The only person who doesn't call me Crash is a hambone named Penn. Stupid name, stupid kid. Calls himself a Quaker. Only Quaker I know about is the Quaker Oats cereal. Penn says being a Quaker is somebody who doesn't believe in violence.

Tell me, how can a guy named Crash hang out with a guy who is nonviolent? Stick around to find out.

Spinelli, Jerry. **The Library Card.** Scholastic, 1997, 148pp. Grades 4 & Up.

Realistic fiction. *African Americans; friendship; hobbies; men's issues; peer pressure.*

Weasel could not figure out his best friend, Mongoose. They used to be as close as brothers. They used to enjoy the same things, like painting graffiti on trees, houses, schools, whatever.

One day Weasel follows Mongoose to see what's up with his bro'. Mongoose is hanging out in the library! Weasel remembered how odd Mongoose had been acting lately. Mongoose was saying dumb things about insects, birds, and whales. Now Mongoose says he doesn't want to quit school after all.

The worst thing happened the other day. Mongoose walked by Weasel without speaking because he had his nose in a book!

How can a book be more important than a bro'?

Spinelli, Jerry. **Maniac Magee.** Dell, 1990, 184pp. Grades 5 & Up. A Newbery Award and Young Readers' Choice Award winner.

Realistic fiction. *African Americans; homeless; interracial relations; orphans; racism; runaways.*

Maniac Magee is a legend.

Maniac is a homeless, teenage orphan. He moves from one family to another, from black to white, back and forth like a yo-yo.

Each time he leaves, he does something so remarkable that he adds to his legend. Once he ran like the wind on the railroad tracks–so fast people thought he might have been a running ghost. What about the time he untied a huge knot in Cobble's Corner? It took him three days to do it. For a while he lived in a zoo and slept with the buffalo!

Maniac Magee is a legend. Find out why.

Spinelli, Jerry. **There's a Girl in My Hammerlock.** (Pbk.) S & S Trade, 1991, 208pp. Grades 5 & Up.

Sports. *Love; sports; women's issues.*

What's that again? There's a girl in my hammerlock?

You heard right.

Maisie Potter is definitely a girl and has just joined the wrestling team. It's the only way that Maisie can get close to Eric–even if it is in a hammerlock!

Maisie never expects to get so much attention from the wrestling coach and the school. She even has an article written about her in the local newspaper.

Maisie learns about herself, too. She learns she has more courage than strength. She learns her best friend means more to her than Eric. And, well, lots of things I don't have time to go into. Read this humorous book about the girl in the hammerlock.

Spinelli, Jerry. **Wringer.** HarperCollins, 1997, 229pp. Grades 5 & Up. A Newbery Honor book.

Realistic fiction. *Ethics; men's issues; peer pressure; rites of passage.*

"Dad, were you a wringer?"

Palmer's dad looks at him. "Yep."

"Will I be a wringer, too?"

Palmer's dad nods. "Sure thing, big guy. When you're 10."

A wringer breaks the neck of injured pigeons on Pigeon Day. Five thousand pigeons are released that day to be shot as a sport. The thought of killing pigeons horrifies Palmer. He wonders why he has to kill something to become a man.

What would his Dad say if he knew Palmer has a pet pigeon named Nipper? Would Palmer be less of a man?

Stolz. Mary. **A Dog on Barkham Street.** Illustrated by Leonard Shortall. HarperTrophy, 1968, 184pp. Grades 4-6. First in a series: **The Bully of Barkham Street** and **The Explorer of Barkham Street** follow.

Realistic fiction. *Abuse; animals (dogs); ethics; men's issues; responsibility.*

Note: *This series is excellent and still in print, although the books were written some time ago. The topic is timely because children are still tormented by bullies. The following book, **The Bully on Barkham Street**, tells the story from Marvin's viewpoint; this book could help children understand what motivates a bully to torment others. The last book, **The Explorer of Barkham Street**, tells of Marvin's growing up and maturing.*

How can you avoid a bully if he lives next door? How can you throttle him if he's two years older and bigger?

That is one problem Edward Frost has. One big problem. Edward also wants to own a dog, but his parents say he is not responsible enough to take care of a pet. Two big problems.

When his Uncle Josh comes for a visit, things start to change. First, Uncle Josh owns a beautiful dog named Argess. Then, Uncle Josh has a strategy that just might work with the bully Marvin. Uncle Josh writes a sign that reads, "My bike can lick your bike," and tells Edward to place it on Marvin's handlebars. When Marvin sees the sign, he actually laughs!

The only trouble is that Uncle Josh is a drifter who moves from place to place. What will happen when he leaves and takes his dog with him?

Taylor, Theodore. **Timothy of the Cay.** Harcourt Brace, 1993, 161pp. Grades 4-7. This book is a prequel-sequel to **The Cay.**

Realistic fiction. *African Americans; Caribbean and Latin America; class conflict; death; interracial relations; racism; survival.*

Note: *Explain to the students what a "prequel" is and what a "sequel" is. Then tell them that this book is unusual because it has both. The chapters jump back and forth in time as it reveals Timothy's earlier life–a prequel–to Phillip's life after being rescued–a sequel.*

I am Phillip Enright. I'm 12 years old and I'm blind.

My blindness helps me see many things. For example, I see Timothy Bumbs as wise and kind instead of as an old, black seafarer. I see that a wise person is different from an educated person.

When Timothy and I were shipwrecked and stranded on a desert island, we learned how to survive and how to love each other. Unfortunately, I am the only survivor. Timothy will always be my guardian angel, no matter what my mother says or thinks.

This operation may restore my eyesight. I want to be able to see so I can go back to the cay and see where Timothy is buried. Can my dream be realized?

Temple, Frances. **Grab Hands and Run.** Orchard Books, 1993, 165pp. Grades 5 & Up.

Realistic fiction. *Caribbean and Latin America; runaways; survival.*

"If they come for me, take the children. Grab hands and run. Go north, all the way to Canada. If I ever get free, I'll come there."

These words were spoken to Felipe's mother late one night. Felipe's father knew the danger. He had already been arrested twice for his political beliefs.

Soon after the conversation, Felipe's father is missing, and his motorcycle is found abandoned. Felipe, his mother, and his sister grab hands and run. They run from their home in El Salvador to freedom in Canada. They flee from fire, flood, snakes, and bullets.

Maybe one day Felipe's father can join them.

Wallace, Bill. **Blackwater Swamp.** Holiday House, 1994, 185pp. Grades 4-6.

Mysteries/thrillers. *Crime; ethics; supernatural; trust.*

Beware of the witch of Blackwater Swamp!

At first Ted thought the witch of Blackwater Swamp was an urban legend. It was just a scary story repeated to kids to give them nightmares.

Then Ted saw the witch for himself. She was just as scary looking as all the stories said. She kept cages around the swamp like the witch did in the folktale Hansel and Gretel. Maybe the witch would try to eat Ted!

Ted knew he should obey the witch's warning to "git!" and "go home!" but he had to discover the truth. Was the witch responsible for the recent thefts that occurred in his town?

Who is this witch of Blackwater Swamp? Ted finds out, and now so can you.

Watkins, Yoko Kawashima. **My Brother, My Sister and I.** Simon & Schuster, 1994, 275pp. Second in a series: **So Far from the Bamboo Grove** precedes.

Biography. *Asia (Japan); death; orphans; rites of passage; survival; World War II.*

 Note: This biography demonstrates that the Japanese also suffered in World War II. This is a good companion book to Sook Nyui Choi's series (on pages 15, 50, 51) because both books describe the horrors of the same war from different points of view.

Life was hard in Japan in 1947. We Japanese had lost the war and suffered many casualties due to the atomic bomb. It was a time of survival of the fittest.

My family was luckier than most. True, my mother died from stress and my father was missing. Yet I had my older brother, Hideyo, and my older sister, Ko. Together we endured starvation, humiliation, and slander by our jealous neighbors.

My brother, my sister, and I want to share our story with you.

Wright, Betty Ren. **The Dollhouse Murders.** Scholastic, 1983, 149pp. Grades 3-5. A Young Readers' Choice Award winner.

Horror. *Crime; disability (mental); revenge; secrets; supernatural.*

 Note: There is a subplot of a mentally impaired younger sister that is touching and sensitive. This book is an excellent read-aloud.

Amy and her friend Ellen are fascinated by Aunt Clare's dollhouse in the attic. It is a replica of the house in which Aunt Clare and Amy's dad once lived. There are even dolls that resemble the family.

Aunt Clare insists that she and her brother had unhappy memories living with their grandparents, but she refuses to talk about them. Whenever the dollhouse is mentioned, she becomes upset. Something about that dollhouse is certainly strange.

What happened that made Aunt Clare so unhappy about her past? Why did the dolls keep moving when no one was in the attic? Why did the light turn on and off in the dollhouse?

Amy decides to become a detective to find out for herself.

Yep, Laurence. **Dragon's Gate.** HarperCollins, 1993, 277pp. Grades 6 & Up.

Historical fiction. *Asian Americans; immigrants; interracial relations; racism; rites of passage; survival; work.*

Note: This book can also be recommended to older readers.

Strange how your life can turn around in a single moment. What if I hadn't gone to that restaurant? What if I hadn't even gone to see the Dragon's Gate?

I certainly would not have accidentally killed that Manchu soldier. Then I would not have escaped from my homeland in China to join my father and uncle in California. I would not be joining them to work on the great transcontinental railroad. I would not be trying to chisel a path through the Sierra Nevada Mountains.

Driven to despair, I have no choice but to take on this desperate and dangerous mission that may claim my life. I must dynamite an area to start an avalanche. That is the only way I can gain back my freedom.

How I wish I could turn back the hands of time and begin again.

Zindel, Paul. **Loch.** HarperCollins, 1994, 209pp. Grades 4 & Up.

Horror. *Ecology; supernatural; survival.*

The Loch Ness monster is alive!

I know you've been told the Loch Ness monster is a myth. You've probably been told those photographs are fake. Cavenger and his crew will strongly disagree with you. They've seen the creature they call Rogue. Rogue has even eaten their cameraman!

If this isn't enough, another plot is hatching without Cavenger's knowledge. Lock and Zaidee are the son and daughter of a marine biologist on Cavenger's ship. They discover Rogue's offspring, whom they call Wee Beastie.

They want Wee Beastie alive. Cavenger wants Rogue dead.

What will be the outcome?

CHAPTER

3

Booktalks for the
Middle School (Grades 6-9)

Middle school can begin at different
grades, from the fifth to seventh
grades. Regardless of the grade, this
group of booktalks will deal with the difficul-
ties of adolescence. Some of the books may
contain profanity, but sexual topics will be dis-
creetly mentioned. Recommend these books to
advanced readers in both middle and high
school. Of course, each student is different,
and some of the topics may be offensive. When
booktalking to students, warn them about any
controversial topics, then let them choose.
They usually know what they can handle.

Most of the these selected books haven't
dated over time. However, many young adult
books do have a short book life, approximately
10 years or less, because they refer to details
such as clothing, slang, and music. Only some
authors, such as Lois Duncan, will appeal to
teenagers more than 20 years later. For this

reason, buy paperbacks or bound paperbacks.
You should then be able to buy multiple copies
of favorites.

Another reason to buy paperbacks is that
teenagers may store books in bookbags out of
sight from their critical peers. Reading is not
considered "cool" by many of their peers. We
should realize this and try to overcome this
prejudice. Because peer pressure is so important, you might consider using a display of
student-recommended books. Students can
also booktalk their favorites. This knowledge
helps us learn something of their reading atti-
tudes and interests.

Although books and authors seem to
change as frequently as the styles, one theme
that endures in young adult literature is the
search for self-identity. Almost all of the books
in this chapter deal with this theme. Another
theme that frequently appears is taking

responsibility, perhaps because this trait is a requirement for becoming a mature person.

Multicultural books are important for adolescents. For many students, they will only be exposed to different cultures and races through books. The more exposed they are to different cultures, the more tolerant they will become. There are also students who will identify with the various cultures and need books to reaffirm their self-identity.

With this age, you may detect a more emotional and inflated response about books. Comments on the same book might range from "I hated that book!" to "That's the best book I've ever read in my life." Just keep in mind Rosenblatt's theory of "reader response" (*Literature as Exploration*, Modern Language Association, 1938). Each reader brings a per-

sonal history and background to each book. That's why we as educators shouldn't be offended if a book we loved does not appeal to someone else. Teenagers are more vocal about their choices and use descriptive language to express themselves.

As in Chapters 2 and 4, book awards are mentioned, but this is not an extensive search. Along with the Newbery and Carnegie awards, there are some other notable awards. The ALA Best Book for Young Adults is annual list compiled by a selected ALA committee of young adult specialists. The Senior Readers' Choice Award is selected by young adults in the Northern states and Canada.

Avi. Nothing but the Truth: A Documentary Novel. Orchard, 1991, 192pp. Grades 7 & Up. An ALA Best Books for Young Adults selection.

Realistic fiction. *Ethics; politics; responsibility.*

Note: This book is an excellent addition to any class discussing freedom of speech and the Constitution.

Do you swear to tell the truth, the whole truth, and nothing but the truth?

What if you don't know the truth? In this book no one knows the truth. That's because no one knows the true story.

The story begins when Phillip Mallory hums the national anthem during Miss Narwin's homeroom class. Phillip is taunting Miss Narwin because she had given him a "D" in English. That bad grade prevents Phillip from playing sports. Unfortunately, no one knows this except Phillip, and this lack of information sets off a chain of events.

Eventually Phillip's parents, the school principal, and a politician become involved. All have their agenda, but no one knows the real truth.

What is the truth? The author Avi brings you the whole truth and nothing but the truth.

Avi. Romeo and Juliet Together (and Alive!) at Last. (Pbk.) Orchard Books, 1987, 128pp. Grades 6 & Up. Second in a series: **S.O.R. Losers** precedes.

Humor. *Friendship; love; peer pressure; revenge; school.*

Note: This is a good read-aloud as well as highly recommended for advanced elementary readers.

It all begins when shy Pete Saltz falls for Annabelle Stackpoole. It all ends with the eighth grade class production of Shakespeare's *Romeo and Juliet.* Scattered throughout is much humor as one hilarious disaster after another occurs.

Pete's best friend Ed Siltrow cooks up the idea of producing the play to bring Pete and Annabelle together. Ed's romantic scheme brings its share of problems. The class bully insists on taking a lead role of Romeo. Teachers and parents want to become involved. And who is the wise guy who sets off the firecracker on opening night?

Oh well, all's well that ends well–especially if it brings *Romeo and Juliet Together (and Alive!) at Last!*

Avi. Wolf Rider. Collier, 1993, 202pp. Grades 5 & Up.

Mysteries/thrillers. *Crime; illness (mental); revenge; suicide; survival.*

"I just killed someone."

Andy tries to keep the anonymous killer talking on the telephone while a friend runs next door to contact the police. "Really? Whom did you kill?"

"I killed Nina."

That mysterious phone call led Andy on an investigation to find the caller and Nina. As it turns out, Nina may not be the only target for murder!

Banks, Lynn Reid. **Melusine: A Mystery.** HarperCollins Children's Books, 1989, 204pp. (Pbk.) HarperCollins, 1991, 201pp. Grades 7-9.

Mysteries/thrillers. *Europe (France); love; occult; supernatural.*

Note: This book is both a romance and supernatural thriller. Also, you might remind students that the author is the creator of the **Indian in the Cupboard** series.

Have you ever made friends with a ghost? Maybe you have and didn't know it!

Roger had no idea Melusine was a ghost when he met her. He only knew she was the most beautiful girl he had ever seen. He and his family were staying at an old French chateau, hoping to learn some French culture. They never suspected the place was haunted. Okay, the chateau did look a bit spooky with the overgrown vines and ramshackle appearance, but that's to be expected. Isn't it?

Monsieur Serpe was a bit strange, with his curt manner and secretive ways. However, it was Melusine, his milkmaid daughter, who was very odd. She had an unusual manner of gliding and then disappearing.

Melusine told Roger about the toweróa secret place that he was forbidden to enter. Somehow he knew this tower was the answer to the riddle of Melusine.

Baron, Nick. **Virtual Destruction.** (Pbk.) Zebra, 1995, 219pp. Grades 7-9.

Horror. *Computers; men's issues; peer pressure; problem parents; rites of passage; survival.*

Marc McClaren is addicted to video games. He can't believe he has been selected to preview an awesome virtual reality game.

After his preview, he begins having nightmares. Weird accidents start to happen. One by one, his friends die.

It occurs to Marc that this virtual reality game has become his reality. Now he has to work out a way to end the game before it ends him!

Bauer, Joan. **Squashed.** Delacorte, 1992, 194pp. Grades 7-9. An ALA Best Books for Young Adults selection.

Romance. *Hobbies; love; responsibility.*

"Have you hugged your pumpkin today? Well, at least talk to it!"

That piece of horticultural advice comes from Wes, the boy whom Ellie admires from afar. This humorous account occurs under the shade of a 200-pound pumpkin named Max.

Ellie wants two things out of life: to win the Rock River Pumpkin Weigh-In Contest and to win Wes's heart. Wes helps Max grow into the biggest pumpkin in the history of the contest.

Many funny and exciting things happen as the pumpkin grows. Get *Squashed* by Joan Bauer.

Bauer, Joan. **Thwonk.** Delacorte, 1995, 215pp. Grades 7-9. An ALA Best Books for Young Adults selection.

Romance. *Love; magic; school.*

A. J. McCreary can't help herself. She has a gigantic crush on Peter Terris, the best-looking guy in her school. Peter is in love with Julia and doesn't even know A. J. exists.

One magical day A. J. meets a cupid, named Jonathan, who agrees to help her in only one of three ways: either artistically, academically, or romantically. A. J. chooses a romantic wish.

Thwonk!

The arrow strikes Peter and he is embarrassingly fixated on A. J. He loudly proclaims his love for her, even in front of the school principal. Peter has become human Super Glue.

How can A. J. shake off Peter and get back to her normal unromantic life?

Beake, Lesley. **Song of Be.** Henry Holt, 1993, 94pp. Grades 6 & Up.

Realistic fiction. *Africa; death; illness (mental); interracial relations; racism; responsibility; suicide.*

 The opening of the book is intentionally shocking. I paraphrased the beginning. However, Be does not kill herself and comes to a resolution of her problems. Lesley Beake is an award-winning South African author.

I have just killed myself.

I tried to pierce the vein of my arm with a poison arrow. I was shaking, so that the arrow tip went into the thickest part of my leg. Perhaps this gives me time to think.

Who am I? I am Be, of the Ju/'hoan people. I am known to many as a member of the Bushmen tribe, living in Namibia.

Why do I want to die? Maybe I need to remember before I finally die. Maybe then I'll be clean of things that happened last summer.

Maybe then I can rest forever.

Bell, William. **Forbidden City.** Bantam Books, 1990, 199pp. Grades 6 & Up.

Historical fiction. *China; class conflict; politics; survival.*

 You might need to give background on the student uprising in Beijing in 1989. The famous photograph of the student facing the tank has become an icon that could be shown as part of the booktalk.

Awesome. Here I am, Alex Jackson, off to China with my dad. My dad is a camera operator for the Canadian Broadcasting Corporation. He plans to film Russian Premier Gorbachev making an official visit to China.

I didn't realize we would come during the student and citizen demonstrations in Tiananmen Square in Beijing. I didn't realize that I would become a reporter of these events. I didn't think my Dad would be captured by the military police. I didn't realize I would be a witness to violence, dissension, and even death.

How can we get home safely?

Bennet, Jay. **Skinhead.** (Pbk.) Fawcett Juniper, 1991, 146pp. Grades 6-9.

Mysteries/thrillers. *Crime; death; love; revenge; secrets; survival.*

 Note: All of Jay Bennett's books are good recommendations for students who like horror and mystery.

The telephone rang. Jonathan Atwood picked up the receiver. "Jonathan Atwood? Go back home. If you don't go home, you'll die. Just like that man in the park did. He wasn't a pretty sight, was he? This is your final warning."

After that telephone call, Jonathan has every intention of leaving Seattle. Then he meets Jenny Mason, who has vital information about the victim. Now Jonathan can never leave–no matter what happens!

Block, Francesca Lia. **Missing Angel Juan.** HarperCollins, 1993, 138pp. Grades 8 & Up. An ALA Best Books for Young Adults selection. Fourth in series: **Weetzie Bat; Witch Baby;** and **Cherokee Bat and the Goat Guys** precede; **Be Bop Baby** follows.

Realistic fiction. *Love; occult; rites of passage; sex and sexuality; supernatural.*

Note: The author's stream of consciousness style is appealing to some teenagers. Many readers enjoy the complete series.

I thought Angel Juan Perez and Witch Baby Secret Agent Wigg Bat would be together forever. I was wrong.

I have pictures of Angel Juan everywhere on my bedroom walls. Angel Juan the hopeful rock star. Angel Juan kissing the sky. Angel Juan the blur doing hip-hop moves. Angel Juan and his Witch Baby hugging their cactus Sunshine. I never thought Angel Juan would go away. But he did, saying that "nothing feels safe."

No choice. I split for New York to find Angel Juan. Instead I find the ghost of my best friend and almost grandfather Charlie Bat. We go all over the city to find Angel Juanójust that ghost and me.

Do we find Angel Juan? That's for me to know and for you to find out!

Bloor, Edward. **Tangerine.** Harper Brace, 1997, 294pp.; (Pbk.) Apple, 1998, 289pp. Grades 6 & Up. An ALA Best Books for Young Adults selection.

Realistic fiction. *Disability (physical); ecology; interracial relations; men's issues; rivalry; sports (football and soccer).*

I'll admit it. I'm afraid of my older brother, Erik. He's dangerous.

I'm not scared of many things. I'm a goalie in soccer and I'm diagnosed as legally blind. Obviously, I'm not a coward.

Somehow my brother does scare me. He'll do anything to achieve his "Erik Fisher Football Dream." He thinks he is God's gift to humanity because he's a star kicker on his team. If his threats don't work, he has this psycho friend, Arthur, who carries a blackjack.

Another thing about Erik is that he has something to do with my loss of eyesight. I can't remember how, but these flashbacks keep popping up in my mind.

What is it about Erik I'm too scared to remember?

Brooks, Martha. **Two Moons in August.** Little, Brown, 1991, 199pp. Grades 6-9. An ALA Best Books for Young Adults selection.

Realistic fiction. *Death; illness (physical); love; trust.*

What can I tell you about my mom? That she was young, pretty, and vibrant until she contracted tuberculosis and died last year? Enough said. I don't like to think or talk about her too much. It's just too painful.

I can tell you about this strange boy I just met. I'm always doing something dumb around him–tripping, being nasty, acting crazy. If I didn't know better, I would say I'm in love with Kieran McMorran.

So, how do Kieran and my dead mom get all linked in my mind? I'm going crazy trying to figure this all out.

Maybe you can help me. Read *Two Moons in August* and see what you think.

Byars, Betsy. **The Summer of the Swans.** Illustrated by Ted CaConis. Viking Kestral, 1970, 142pp. Grades 4-7. A Newbery Award winner.

Realistic fiction. *Death; disability (mental); rites of passage.*

> Note: *This Newbery winner is hard to categorize because it can also be read to younger audiences. However, Sara is definitely going through adolescence so I placed in the middle school section.*

This has been the worst summer of my life. One minute I'm happy, the next minute I'm sad. One minute I love my orange sneakers, then I want to dye them blue. I'm like a seesaw, up and down, down and up.

Things haven't been right since Mother died. After her death, Wanda, Charlie, and I moved in with Aunt Willie. My sister Wanda now has a boyfriend, named Frank. Vomit. My brother Charlie is the same, but he's always the same. He's called mentally retarded, something I never call him. As for me, I'm so mixed up, so moody.

When Charlies disappears, all my moodiness evaporates. Where has he gone? For some reason, I keep thinking he's gone to see the swans by the lake. The day before, Charlie and I went to see the swans, and I could hardly tear him away.

Joe Melby volunteered to help find Charlie. I hate him. Once, I think he stole Charlie's wristwatch just to torment him. I hate anyone who mocks Charlie.

If I do find Charlie, I promise not to get all bent out of shape over stupid things like dyeing my sneakers another color. Never, never, never again.

Cannon, A. E. **Amazing Gracie.** Dell, 1991, 214pp. Grades 7 & Up.

Realistic fiction. *Eating disorders; illness (mental depression); responsibility; single parents; substance abuse.*

Amazing Gracie, that's me. I can accomplish amazing things. I can cook, clean, pay bills, and babysit my six-year-old stepbrother. Most of all, I take care of my depressed mom.

Taking care of my mom is my main priority. Sometimes she won't eat, sleep or take her medication. Then I have to be the adult.

Well, I'm tired of being the adult. I want to be a regular teenager with dates and fun. I'm sick of being Amazing Gracie.

Carter, Alden R. **Between a Rock and a Hard Place.** Scholastic, 1995, 211pp. Grades 7 & Up. An ALA Best Books for Young Adults selection.

Adventure. *Illness (physical); men's issues; rites of passage; survival; trust.*

> *Note:* This exciting book is similar to Paulsen's **Hatchet,** *but this book contains strong profanity. You might warn the audience of this.*

It's a family tradition. It's sort of a rite-of-passage. During adolescence the Severson guys go camping at the dangerous Boundary Waters. Mark's dad, Uncle Jerry, and his brother did it years ago. Now it's Mark's turn. Mark's cousin Randy will go along, too.

It wasn't supposed to turn out so badly. First of all, Randy is a diabetic and loses his insulin. Then Mark loses his compass in the water. Neither of the boys have any camping skills whatsoever. Now they are lost without a canoe, food, and shelter. All they can depend on is each other.

Mark and Randy are between a rock and a hard place. Will they survive?

Childress, Alice. **Rainbow Jordon.** Avon Faire, 1982, 128pp. Grades 7 & Up.

Realistic fiction. *African Americans; problem parents; racism; secrets; self-identity.*

Name's Rainbow Jordon. I tell the kids to call me Rainey and that it stands for Laraine. Lottsa kids razz me about that Rainbow stuff. Nobody in the world named that. One boy says, "You too dark to be a Rainbow. They shoulda called you Stormcloud."

Never mind. Mom—I mean Kathie—named me that when she was 15 years old. She was just a babe in arms herself. Now she some sort of fan dancer. I tell people Miz Josie, the lady I live with, is my aunt. Don't want to put all our business in the street.

Lotta people will mouth your business to the world if they ever peep into your personal secrets. Sometime it be hard to keep secrets. Like when I went to the circus and saw a man walking the high wire and keeping his balance. Ha! Ask me about it. I do it every day.

Choi, Sook Nyul. **Echoes of the White Giraffe.** Houghton Mifflin, 1993, 137pp. Grades 5-8. Second in a series: **The Year of Impossible Years** precedes; **Gathering of Pearls** follows.

Historical fiction. *Asia (Korea); love; rites of passage; World War II.*

> *Note:* see page 15 for the booktalk on the first book in the series. Both middle and elementary readers enjoy this series.

Sookan, the unforgettable Korean heroine of *The Year Of Impossible Goodbyes,* is now 15 years old. She and her family are refugees in Pusan, a city in South Korea. Sookan, her mother, and her brother are waiting for news of her father and older brothers.

In the meantime she meets Junho, a handsome boy who sings with her in the church choir. They develop a close friendship. However, something unfortunate happens. A photograph of the two is discovered, and this photograph scandalizes both of the families. Sookan is forbidden to see Junho again.

Should Sookan continue her relationship with Junho knowing she is ruining her reputation?

Choi, Sook Nyul. **Gathering of Pearls.** Houghton Mifflin, 1994, 163pp. Grades 6 & Up. Third in a series: **The Year of the Impossible Goodbyes** and **Echoes of the White Giraffe** precede.

Historical fiction. *Asian Americans; death; interracial relations; rites of*

"Yes, I don't like it." Sookan Bak says the English words carefully to her college roommate. Sookan's thoughts are in Korean, and she still finds English confusing. Now Sookan is living in America, attending Finch College.

Sookan has lived through so much in her young life. In Korea she escaped from the Japanese and Russian soldiers, and located her missing mother. Learning the strange American ways is another test for Sookan. What does "going Dutch" mean? Why do some men do women's work, like cooking? Why do Americans marry for love and not obligation?

When problems occur, Sookan remembers her mother's words: "Tough times are the times when one gathers one's pearls." Sookan vows to gather her pearls. She will finish college and make her family proud of her.

Cleary, Beverly. **A Girl from Yamhill: A Memoir.** Dell, 1988; (Pbk.) Dell, 1989, 320pp. Grades 6 & Up. First in a series: **My Own Two Feet: A Memoir** follows.

Biography. *Hobbies; love; problem parents; rites of passage.*

Meet the author of the series about *Ramona*, the *Mouse and the Motorcycle*, and *Henry Huggins*. She's one of the funniest writers around.

You might be surprised to learn that her early life was not humorous. She had many problems that some of you have. She didn't get along with her mother. She moved into a new community and school. She didn't feel attractive or special.

Born in 1916, Beverly Bunn came from pioneer ancestors and lived on a farm in Yamhill, Oregon. Later she moved to Portland. She won her first writing contest in elementary school. Guess why she won? She was the only one who entered the contest!

She ends her book after high school and continues in her sequel, *My Own Two Feet.* I think you'll find a dark side in this girl from Yamhill, the writer we know as Beverly Cleary.

Cole, Brock. **The Goats.** Farrar, Strauss & Giroux, 1987, 184pp. Grades 7 & Up. An ALA Best Books for Young Adults selection.

Realistic fiction. *Ethics; peer pressure; runaways; survival.*

We are the Goats. We are the misfits of the Tall Pine camp. It's a camp tradition to strip us Goats of our clothes and to leave us marooned on a deserted island for a night.

I'm Laura the Goat. You will also meet Howie, the other Goat. Together, we decide to swim ashore and disappear completely. We want to give the campers a little scare of their own.

Note: This book is reminiscent of another classic novel that speaks to young people—**Lord of the Flies.** Perhaps you could recommend this one as well.

Collier, James & Christopher. The Clock. Illustrated by Kelly Maddox. Delacorte, 1992, 162pp. Grades 6 & Up.

Historical fiction. *Sexual abuse; work; women's issues.*

In 1810 there were no terms such as child abuse, unsafe working conditions, and sexual harassment. Yet these problems existed in 1810. There just were no laws or unions to protect the workers. In 1810 it was especially unsafe for pretty young girls to work in the mills.

Annie Steele is forced to work in a Connecticut mill. Her shiftless father refuses to provide for his family. She must endure low wages with the threat of being beaten by the cruel overseer, Mr. Hoggart.

Mr. Hoggart has taken a liking to the pretty Annie. Neither her orphan friend, Tom, nor her neighbor, Robert, can protect her. Annie's family doesn't believe her. Annie is trapped in a heartless environment.

How does Annie survive?

Try setting *The Clock* on your nightstand.

Colman, Carolyn. Tell Me Everything. Farrar, Strauss & Giroux, 1993, 156pp. Grades 7-9. An ALA Best Books for Young Adults selection.

Realistic fiction. *Death; secrets; sex and sexuality.*

Roz knew her mother did not die on the space shuttle *Challenger*, even if that's what she wrote on her school report. No, her mother died rescuing a young boy. So what? Her mother was just as much a heroine as the astronauts from the *Challenger*. Her mother was a heroine, even though she could be, well, a bit crazy at times.

For almost a year, Roz has been calling Nate, the boy her mother died trying to rescue. Roz quickly hangs up each time he answers. Now Nate has an unlisted phone number. Roz must locate Nate before he disappears forever. At last Roz is ready to ask Nate the important question: "How did my mother die?"

When Roz does locate Nate, she will finally have the courage to say, "Tell me everything."

Conford, Ellen. Dear Lovey Hart, I Am Desperate. Little, Brown, 1975, 224pp. Grades 6-9. First in a series: **We Interrupt This Semester for an Important Bulletin** follows.

Romance. Love; peer pressure; school; secrets.

Cassie Wasserman is Lovey Hart, the anonymous advice columnist for the high school paper. Sometimes it's easier being Lovey Hart than Cassie Wasserman. For instance, Cassie has a crush on Chip Custer, the editor of the paper. It was his idea that she write the column, and that secret is troubling her. Carrie knows that somehow this secret will be discovered by her curious classmates. Then they're certain to make fun of her. After all, if Cassie has no love life, how can she advise others?

Note: In addition, you might read one of Lovey Hart's letters. All of Ellen Conford's books have a light touch that is appealing to young adults. Her books don't date because she writes humorously about teenage romance.

Conford, Ellen. **A Royal Pain.** (Pbk.) Scholastic, 1990, 171pp. Grades 6-9.

Romance. *Love; rivalry; self-identity.*

> *Note:* This is a repetition of the theme of switching identities, as in Mark Twain's **The Prince and the Pauper.**

Would you like to be royalty, to have all your wishes and desires fulfilled? That's what 15-year-old Abby Addams of Kansas thought, too. Then she becomes royalty. Abby discovers it can be a royal pain!

You see, Abby was born in the European country of Saxony. She and Princess Florinda XIV were accidentally switched at birth. Once this is discovered, Abby is sent to Saxony to begin life as a princess.

At first Abby loves being a princess. There are no dishes to wash, no homework, and no irritating parents to tell her what to do. Then Abby discovers she has to marry Prince Casimir, a person she detests on sight. Why, oh, why can't the Prince be the cool reporter who wants to interview her?

Eventually she is determined to abdicate the throne. How will she escape? She has no choice. She will have to become a royal pain!

Conly, Jane Leslie. **Crazy Lady!** HarperCollins, 1993, 180pp. Grades 6 & Up. A Newbery Honor book.

Realistic fiction. *Death; disability (mental); substance abuse (alcohol).*

"Crazy lady! Crazy lady!"

That's what we call the old drunk with her retarded son. They're always good for a laugh.

I'm Vernon Dibbs. Sometimes me and my buddies get bored trying to hot wire unlocked cars. That's when we rag old crazy lady Maxine Flooter. We don't mean nothing by it. It's just so funny when the Crazy Lady cusses us, slobbering in the street.

I would never have gotten to know the Crazy Lady if she hadn't asked me about my mom. See, my mom died of a stroke three years ago. I still miss her.

Maybe the Crazy Lady ain't so crazy after all. As I get to know her, I see she loves her son just like my mom loved me, even when I done bad in school and had to repeat a grade. Moms who love like that can't be all crazy, right?

Conrad, Pam. **Stonewords: A Ghost Story.** Scholastic, 1990, 130pp. Grades 5-8.

Horror. *Occult; supernatural; survival; time travel.*

When I met a ghost named Zoe Louise, I knew immediately this had to be the girl from the grave. My mother used to take me to a cemetery and named me after one of the tombstones: Zoe. The rest of the stone words had been chipped away by weather damage. So the name Zoe was all I knew about the poor dead girl.

Later, this ghost Zoe Louise and I became good friends. I became curious just how and when Zoe Louise died. I needed to know what was written on her tombstone, so maybe I could save Zoe Louise from her early death.

What did those stone words say?

Cooney, Caroline B. **Don't Blame the Music.** Putnam, 1986. Grades 6 & Up.

Realistic fiction. *Illness (mental); rivalry.*

"Have faith, honey. Something went terribly wrong with your sister. Maybe it was my fault, and maybe it wasn't. At least let's not blame the music."

That's what my mother says about my crazy sister Ashley. Ashley became an overnight rock star. She had only one hit record and faded away into teen twilight.

I guess I'm the good daughter: nice looking, popular, smart. No one knows my problems at home with my 25-year-old sister, who is a burned out, strung out loony tune.

In order not to go crazy myself, I write my thoughts and poems in my journal. One day my journal is gone. Missing.

Who has my journal? Who is reading it? Is it Carmine or Whit from the high school rock band Crude Oil? Is it my best friend, Emily? Is it my enemy, Shepherd?

Who will discover the real me?

Cooney, Caroline B. **Driver's Ed.** Delacorte, 1994, 184pp. Grades 6 & Up. An ALA Best Books for Young Adults selection; a Senior Readers' Choice Award winner.

Realistic fiction. *Death; peer pressure; rites of passage.*

 Based on a true story, this book discusses an important issue among teenagers–assuming responsibility.

The television announcer read this report:

"A car driven by 26 year old Denise Thompson was hit broadside by a truck. Denise Thompson was killed instantly. A stop sign was missing on Cherry Hill. She leaves a husband and two small children."

Morgan's heart skipped a beat. His thoughts were whirling. He wondered if this was some kind of nightmare. He tried to tell himself that everyone steals stop signs. They were just having fun. How could this happen?

"Whoever took that sign," said Morgan's father, "should be shot."

Morgan's head throbbed as he remembered something that terrified him.

That stop sign was lying on its side in the garage–in plain view.

Cooney, Caroline B. **The Face on the Milk Carton.** Bantam Doubleday Dell, 1990, 184pp. Grades 6-9. First in a series: **Whatever Happened to Janie?** and **The Voice on the Radio** follow.

Realistic fiction. *Crime; secrets; self-identity; trust.*

Janie Johnson couldn't believe her eyes. Was that little girl on the milk carton really her? Below the picture was a description of a missing three-year-old girl who had been kidnapped 12 years ago from a shopping mall in New Jersey.

Come to think of it, Janie couldn't remember much of her early childhood. Maybe she should do some investigating.

After searching in the attic, Janie discovers a dress with tiny dark polka dots. It was the dress on the milk carton!

Janie has the evidence. Now she wants some answers.

Cooney, Caroline B. **The Fog.** (Pbk.) Scholastic, 1989, 218pp. Grades 6-9. First in a series: **The Snow** and **The Fire** follow.

Horror. *Abuse; crime; death; revenge; survival.*

Do you like books by Stephen King, Christopher Pike, and R. L. Stine? Then this horror series is for you.

The Shevvingtons own a boarding school on a remote island that is approachable only by ferry. Christina is one of the boarding students. She notices that the Shevvingtons have a twisted, cruel side that reveals itself only to the students, never to the parents.

Strange accidents begin to occur. When the Shevvingtons suspect that Christina is suspicious of them, they try to destroy her by fog, snow, and fire.

Will Christina survive the horrible Shevvingtons?

Try this series. It will just kill you!

Cooney, Caroline B. **The Girl who Invented Romance.** (Pbk.) Bantam, 1988, 167pp. Grades 7-9.

Romance. *Love; peer pressure; school.*

Have you ever played the game *Romance*?

I mean, have you ever played the board game of Romance? Romance promises to be the latest and greatest game of the year.

One day Kelly was talking to her best friends about her lackluster romantic life. She got an idea to invent a board game called *Romance*, with all the rules that you would use in real life. Maybe the game would teach Kelly how to attract Will's attention.

When Kelly invites a dozen of her friends over her house to play *Romance*, she begins her own romance. Will she live happily ever after? Ask the girl who invented *Romance.*

Cooney, Caroline B. **Twenty Pageants Later.** Bantam, 1991. Grades 7 & Up.

Realistic fiction. Hobbies; rivalry; women's issues.

Twenty pageants later Dane McShane calls herself a professional at winning beauty contests.

Dane knows all the right things to do or say. A contestant must develop a talent that flatters her beauty. Blowing a trumpet is taboo because it spoils your looks. The contestant should speak sweetly, even when the emcee is an inexperienced jerk. A contestant must refrain from unprofessional behavior, such as waving to your family in the audience.

Let Dane share all her beauty secrets twenty pageants later.

Cooney, Caroline B. **Whatever Happened to Janie?** Delacorte, 1993, 199pp. Grades 7-9. Second in a series: **The Face on the Milk Carton** precedes; **The Voice on the Radio** follows.

Realistic fiction. Crime; problem parents; rivalry; self-identity; trust.

Whatever happened to Janie, the face on the milk carton?

Janie Johnson is now Jennie Spring. She is back with her natural parents after a 12-year separation. When Janie or Jennie was three-years-old, she had been kidnapped from a shopping mall. She discovered a picture of her face on a milk carton declaring her as missing. She took the proper search to find her natural parents.

Even though the mystery of the kidnapping has been solved, the nightmare continues. Janie or Jennie must cope with four siblings who resent her. Her natural mother and father don't seem to know how to love her.

Janie Johnson or Jennie Spring? Which one is she?

Cross, Gillian. **Chartbreak.** Oxford Press, 1986, 181pp. Grades 7-9.

Realistic fiction. Music; *show business; work.*

As a reporter for a rock magazine, I had the opportunity to interview the singer Finch from the rock band Kelp. It was quite an experience.

Born Janis Mary Finch in Birmingham, England, Finch joined Kelp after getting "in a row with my Mum and her mate." She said the concert in Nottingham when the band supported Nitrogen Cycle was their launching pad. "That's when everything came 100% right for the first time. An amazing feeling," Finch said enthusiastically.

Finch groaned when I asked her about the band's first-ever Top of the Pop television appearance. Viewers are still talking about that controversial performance. Finch waved off the question with her tattooed hand. "Look, there's no way I can tell you in a couple of words. I have to go back to the beginning. To find out my story, read *Chartbreak* by Gillian Cross."

Cross, Gillian. **New World.** Holiday House, 1994, 171pp. Grades 7-9.

Horror. Computers; crime; ethics; rivalry; secrets.

Miriam and Stuart have been selected to test a virtual reality game called *New World.*

At first entering the virtual reality of *New World* is exciting to Miriam. Her home life was hectic and school was utterly boring. Then strange things begin to happen. How did the creator know about Miriam's reoccurring nightmares? How did the creator find out about Stuart's fear of spiders? Why were these terrifying elements contained within the game?

Looks like there is danger in this *New World!*

Gillian Cross. **Wolf.** Holiday, 1991, 144pp.; (Pbk.) Scholastic, 1993. Grades 7-9.

Mysteries/thrillers. *Crime; problem parents; revenge.*

One night it is no longer possible to keep the wolf from the door. Mysterious footsteps come softly to the house of Cassy's grandmother. The next day Cassy is sent to live with her irresponsible mother.

At her mother's house Cassy discovers a package hidden in her suitcase. To her horror, she finds the package contains plastic explosives. She also notices a strange creature lurking around the house. Is it her estranged father? Is he a terrorist, as some people say?

Do we have a wolf inside us—a dark, evil side that we try to hide? In *Wolf* find out just who's the big bad wolf.

Crutcher, Chris. **Athletic Shorts: Six Short Stories.** (Pbk.) Dell, 1989, 161pp. Grades 7-9. An ALA Best Books for Young Adults selection.

Sports. *Ethics; interracial relations; men's issues; peer pressure; racism; rivalry; school; sports.*

 Note: Chris Crutcher is an excellent writer who discusses many topics with sports as his main focus. However, he does use profanity. This book is less controversial than some of his others.

I'm Chris Crutcher. I'm the author of young adult books like *Running Loose, The Crazy Electric Game,* and *Chinese Handcuffs.* I am asked what happens to certain characters in my books. My usual answer is, "I haven't the foggiest idea." However, my book of short stories, *Athletic Shorts,* allows me to find out just what's been happening with some of these characters.

For those of you who are familiar with my books and characters, this one's for you. For those of you who don't know me, try on *Athletic Shorts* and see how they fit.

Crutcher, Chris. **Staying Fat for Sarah Byrnes.** Greenwillow, 1993, 216pp. Also published as **The Secrets of Sarah Byrnes.** Grades 7 & Up. An ALA Best Books for Young Adults selection.

Realistic fiction. *Abuse; disability (physical); school; secrets; sports (swimming); trust.*

 Note: This book discusses child abuse in a direct way with some profanity. Sarah eventually escapes from her father with the help of Eric and a counselor.

My name is Eric Calhoune. Most people call me Moby. Strange nickname, I know. The nickname is based on Moby Dick the whale. That's because I'm a swimmer and I look like a whale. If you dressed me up in an orange sweater, you could ride me around the world in 80 days. I'm a blimp off the old block.

Know why I love to swim? Swimming is a thinking man's sport. I also like the waves I create for the guy in the next lane.

Enough about me. As for Sarah Byrnes, she has a condition synonymous with her surname—burns. Her face and hands were badly burned in a mysterious accident. Her father refuses to let Sarah have reconstructive surgery.

Sarah Byrnes and I stick together ever since we developed a case of "terminal uglies." Now, due to my swimming, I'm losing my midriff bulge.

How can I stay her friend and be thin at the same time? I can't. So I'm staying fat for Sarah Byrnes.

Cushman, Karen. **Catherine, Called Birdy.** Clarion, 1994; (Pbk.) HarperTrophy, 1994, 212pp. Grades 6 & Up. A Newbery Honor winner.

Historical fiction. *Great Britain; Middle Ages; rites of passage; women's issues.*

 This book could also be read and enjoyed by elementary students.

19th Day of September, 1290 In the Year of our Lord

I am not your average damsel in distress. True, I do detest my life of weaving, spinning, and sewing. I am near 14 and have never yet seen a hanging. Corpus bones, my life is barren!

However, this maiden does not wish to be rescued by any Master. Once my father selected a rich, middle-aged man for me. When he came to dine, I rubbed my nose until it shone red, blacked out my front teeth with soot, and dressed my hair with mouse bones. All through dinner I smiled a gap-toothed smile and wiggled my ears. To no one's surprise, the Master left without a betrothal.

Now I fear my next problem is more serious. To my displeasure, it seems that my Uncle George and my best friend have fallen in love. What would one use for a magical spell to come between lovers if one has no dragon dung?

Signed: Catherine, called Birdy

Davis, Terry. **If Rock and Roll Were a Machine.** Delacorte, 1992, 209pp. Grades 7-9. An ALA Best Books for Young Adults selection.

Realistic fiction. *Hobbies; men's issues; runaways; school.*

If rock and roll were a machine, it would be a motorcycle. The old bikes, especially the Harleys, make songs by Bob Seger and Bruce Springsteen roar in Bert Bowden's brain.

Burt buys an old Harley-Davidson Sportster from Scotty Shepherd. Now he's on his way to a new life and new identity. He will be a failure no longer. No longer will Burt be humiliated by teachers and parents.

Burt has his machine. Now he's ready to rock and roll out of this town.

Deschamps, Helene. **Spyglass.** Henry Holt, 1995, 308pp. With index. Grades 7 & Up.

Biography. *Death; Europe (France); Jews; love; secrets; survival; World War II.*

My name is Helen Deschamps. I was once a spy.

During World War II, when I was a teenager, I was a spy for the French Resistance and the American OSS. At first it started out like a game. Later I had to renounce family, friends, and any sort of normal lifestyle. Yet, if I had not made that choice, I could not have lived with myself.

This is my story, just as I lived it. Even though I survived, many of my friends did not. This is their story as well.

Dickinson, Peter. **AK.** Victor Gollanez, 1990, 203pp. Grades 7-9.

Realistic fiction. *Africa; death; homeless; men's issues; orphans; war.*

 The African countries are fictional.

"The war was my mother. I'm laying her to rest."

Paul spoke those words as a young orphan who was relocated to the country of Tsheba. He was a warrior because he had fought in the war in Nagala, a small country in Africa. Paul owned an AK. An AK was the most trustworthy gun because it would fire when other guns had jammed or malfunctioned.

How could Paul lay the war to rest—as well as his mighty AK?

Dickinson, Peter. **A Bone from the Dry Sea.** Bantam/Doubleday Books, 1992, 200pp. Grades 6-9. An ALA Best Books for Young Adults selection.

Realistic fiction. *Africa; ecology; rivalry; science; time travel.*

Linnie never dreamed she would go on an archaeological dig in Africa with her dad. She barely knew her dad. Her mom had been divorced from him for ages. He was an anthropologist and stayed away for long periods of time.

When Linnie discovered a bone from the dry sea, she never dreamed it might be of significance. She never thought it would cause conflict between her dad and Dr. Hamiska, the leader of the expedition.

Linnie would never know the true story behind the bone. Four million years ago, a young girl, Li, lived on that spot between the land and the sea. Li enjoyed playing with the dolphins in the area. She kept a bone to remind her of her friendship. Li never knew that bone would be of historic significance four million years later.

Four million years later, Linnie has the bone. She could never have imagined the power of that bone from the dry sea.

Dickinson, Peter. **Eva.** Delacorte, 1989, 219pp. Grades 7 & Up. An ALA Best Books for Young Adults selection.

Fantasy. *Africa; animals (chimpanzees); ecology; science.*

Picture this: You wake up from a coma with a different body.

At 13, Eva has been in a terrible car accident. No longer is she the pretty teenager she remembers.

Her parents try to prepare her for the shock. They explain that it was the only way she could survive. They explain that as zoologists they wanted to try an experiment. Her brain will remain. Only her body has changed.

Still, when Eva looks in the mirror, she is devastated.

Eva is now a chimpanzee!

Dorris, Michael. **The Window.** Hyperion, 1997, 106pp. Grades 7 & Up.

Realistic fiction. *African Americans; interracial relations; Native Americans; problem parents; substance abuse (alcohol).*

Note: This book gives a brief account of Rayona's life as an interracial child of a Native American and an African American. For a more thorough account of Rayona's life, read **A Yellow Raft in Blue Water** by Michael Dorris, contained on page 110.

My parents are more of a problem to me than I am to them.

My mom needs to "dry out" in a treatment center. She used to come in from one of her "hard nights," as she calls them, and declare a "national holiday" for the next day.

My dad is another problem. He's never around except during emergencies.

When my mom took too many "national holidays," my dad sent me to his relatives in Kentucky. I am amazed at my relatives' reaction to me. If they are this fond of me, where were they when I needed unconditional love?

Draper, Sharon M. **Tears of a Tiger.** Atheneum, 1994, 162pp. Grades 8 & Up. A Coretta Scott King Award winner.

Realistic fiction. *African Americans; death; men's issues; responsibility; sports; substance abuse (alcohol); suicide.*

> **Note:** *The author has another book with a frank account of child abuse that uses some of the same characters from this book. However,* **Forged by Fire** *should be recommended to a mature reader. That booktalk is on page 111.*

The local newspaper had a horrifying story about members of the Tigers basketball team:

November 8–Robert Washington, age 17, Captain of the Hazlewood High School basketball team, was killed last night in a fiery automobile accident. Witnesses say the car was driven by Andrew Jackson, 17, also of the Hazlewood team. The car had been noticeably weaving across the lanes of the expressway just before it hit the retaining wall and burst into flames.

After the death of his best friend, Andy cannot get past his guilt and pain. Andy had killed his best friend!

The other passengers, B. J. and Tyrone, seemed to accept the horrible accident. Andy can't seem to get over Robert's death–even in the sympathetic arms of Keisha.

What is a Tiger to do? Cry?

Duncan, Lois. **Daughters of Eve.** (Pbk.) Dell, 1990, 226pp. Grades 7-9.

Horror. *Crime; occult; peer pressure; revenge; supernatural; survival; women's issues.*

> **Note:** *You could slip this booktalk into stationery that says "Congratulations." Don't forget to remind students that Lois Duncan wrote* **I Know What You Did Last Summer** *because they may have seen the horror movie.*

Tammy received this letter:

We are pleased to inform you that you have been selected for membership in Modesta, California, Chapter of Daughters of Eve.

All recipients were thrilled to be selected into the most prestigious and exclusive club in high school.

During the initiation ceremony Tammy had one of her premonitions. The candle spilled blood instead of wax! The next day Tammy withdrew her nomination.

Unfortunately, Ruth, Jane and Laura remained in the Daughters of Eve. This group was sponsored by Irene Stark, a feminist of the highest order. Irene began demanding that the Daughters of Eve commit some deplorable actions–like murder!

Duncan, Lois. **Don't Look Behind You.** (Pbk.) Dell, 1990, 179pp. Grades 7-9.

Mysteries/thrillers. *Crime; revenge; runaways; secrets; survival.*

> **Note:** *This book was published before the real-life murder of Lois Duncan's daughter. See page 112 for a booktalk on the similarities between fact and fiction, in* **Who Killed My Daughter?** *by Lois Duncan.*

Don't look behind you. You may see someone following you. That someone may intend to kill you!

April Corrigan was living an ordinary life until her father testified in court against some drug dealers. The Corrigans were protected by the Federal Witness Protection Program and had to run for their lives. They changed their identifies: their names, their schools, and their future plans.

The Corrigans were warned not to tell anyone about their sudden move out of state. However, April couldn't resist sending her boyfriend a message, starting a chase that may lead to one horrible conclusion–murder!

Duncan, Lois. **Stranger with My Face.** Little Brown, 1981, 166pp. Grades 7-9.

Horror. *Crime; death; love; occult; rivalry; supernatural; survival.*

Laurie had a wonderful summer. She was accepted into the most popular crowd at school. She was also dating Gordon, the leader of the group.

Then strange and weird things begin to occur. First, Gordon swears he saw Laurie with another boy. Laurie knows she was home in bed with the flu. Now the crowd is giving her the cold shoulder. Next, her family and friends begin seeing her in strange places that she wouldn't think of going.

Then Laurie's friends begin having odd accidents. Helen winds up in critical condition from following a stranger who looks like Laurie. Jeff seriously injures himself from following this stranger with Laurie's face.

Laurie wonders, "Is there a stranger with my face?"

Ellis, Carol. **My Secret Admirer.** (Pbk.) Scholastic, 1989, 184pp. Grades 7-9.

Horror. *Abuse; illness (mental); revenge; survival.*

Jenny received a telephone message from her secret admirer:
"You're going to think I'm crazy, Jenny. I am crazy. Crazy about you. Don't laugh. This isn't a joke. Maybe someday I'll be able to tell you face to face. Until then, I'll just keep my eye on you."

At first Jenny was flattered. Then weird things started happening. A dead rattlesnake was left at her door. A motorcycle chased her off a deserted road.

It appeared that Jenny had both a secret admirer and an enemy.

Or could it be that her enemy and her secret admirer were the same person?

Engdahl, Sylvia Louise. **Enchantress from the Stars.** Illustrated by Rodney Shakell. (Pbk.) Macmillan, 1989; Peter Smith, 1991, 275pp. Grades 7 & Up. First book in a series: **The Far Side of Evil** follows. A Newbery Honor book.

Science fiction. *End-of-the-world; ethics; responsibility; science; secrets; war.*

Note: *Sylvia Louise Engdahl's books endure the test of time and are highly recommended for all readers, even if they think they don't enjoy science fiction. For more information about this author and her books, read my article "Enchantress from the Stars: Sylvia Louise Engdahl, Star Trek and Science Fiction" in* The ALAN Review, *Fall 1997.*

Many centuries from now, Elana is a student at the Federation's Anthropological Center. She is studying to become an agent who would seek out new civilizations to explore. Like a *Star Trek* mission, all explorers come in peace. They are under orders never to reveal their identity.

Elana lands on the planet Andrecia. She and other agents try to save the inhabitants from alien Imperial forces. Can this enchantress from the stars save Andrecia from being destroyed?

Try this series by Sylvia Louise Engdahl. It's out of this world!

Farmer, Nancy. **The Ear, the Eye and the Arm.** Puffin Books, 1994, 311pp. Grades 7 & Up. A Newbery Honor book; an ALA Best Books for Young Adults selection.

Mysteries/thrillers. *Africa; occult; revenge; rivalry; supernatural.*

In the year 2194, *The Ear, The Eye and The Arm* is the weirdest detective agency in Zimbabwe. Nobody can do what they can. One detective can hear a bat burp in the basement. One can see a gnat's navel on a foggy night. Another detective can feel hunches that stick like gum to a shoe. These three "gumshoes," or detectives, are genetic mutations.

Enough about them. Let's cut to the chase. Three children are kidnapped and dragged to the underbelly of the city. These are not just any children, mind you, but the children of General Matsika. The General is the most powerful person in Zimbabwe.

Can the kidnapped children escape from the hideous criminals? Will the criminals be captured by *The Ear, The Eye and the Arm?*

Farmer, Nancy. **A Girl Named Disaster.** Orchard Books, 1996, 309pp. Grades 7 & Up. A Newbery Honor book; an ALA Best Books for Young Adults selection.

Realistic fiction. *Abuse; Africa; rites of passage; runaways; supernatural; survival.*

"Nhamo! Selfish, disobedient girl! You have work to do!"

Nhamo always has work to do in her African village in Mozambique. Nhamo's mind is busy as well. Where is her mother's spirit since she was eaten by a leopard? Why did her father disappear? Is there a witch in her village? Why are people dying of cholera?

When the *Muvuki*, or witch-finder, arrives in the village, he declares that Nhamo's father is the cause of the illness. To correct the curse, the witch-finder orders Nhamo to marry a diseased man with several wives.

Nhamo decides to run away. She escapes in a boat down the Mwenezi River to Zimbabwe.

How will this girl named Disaster survive?

Fenner, Carol. **Yolanda's Genius.** Simon & Schuster, 1995, 208pp. Grades 7-9. A Newbery Honor book.

Realistic fiction. *African Americans; disability (mental); interracial relations; self-identity.*

Yolanda is a genius.

Her friend Shirley was the first to call Yolanda a genius. Yolando looked up the word "genius" in the dictionary. She discovered that "true genius rearranges old material in a way never seen before."

Yolanda certainly rearranged the faces of those young thugs who smashed her brother Andrew's harmonica! Yolanda recognizes that her brother Andrew is a genius, too. He can talk through his harmonica. Just because Andrew can't read or write, people think he's stupid. Well, he isn't stupid. He's a genius just like Yolanda.

How can Yolanda convince the world of their genius?

Ferguson, Alane. **Overkill.** Bradbury, 1992, 168pp. Grades 7-9.

Horror. *Crime; illness (mental); occult; revenge; supernatural; survival.*

Those readers who like Lois Duncan's thrillers will probably like this one.

Lacey awakens from her nightmare, shaking and fearful. She had dreamed of her best friend, Celeste, being attacked by someone with a knife.

The next day at school Lacey learns that Celeste was murdered in her home. Just like Lacey's dream, Celeste was stabbed many times.

Did Lacey have some psychic experience? Even more bizarre, maybe it wasn't a dream. Maybe Lacey killed Celeste!

Ferris, Jean. **Relative Strangers.** Farrar, Strauss & Giroux, 1993, 229pp. Grades 7-9.

Realistic fiction. *Europe (France); love; problem parents; stepparents; trust.*

Note: *You can copy these "letters" on appropriate stationery and read the booktalks as letters.*

Dear Berkeley,

I think you're ready to graduate from high school. I want to spend more time with you. After graduation I'd like you to come with me to London and Paris.

By the way, I've recently married again and would like you to meet Paula, my wife.

Your father, Parker Stanton

Dear Mr. Stanton,

I know I won't send this, but these are my honest feelings. I can't call you Dad because I don't know you at all. Lily – or Mom, remember her, the wife you dumped? – says to go on the trip. My boyfriend Spike says to go. He'll be in Europe and we can meet over there. I'm scared to take risks. I think your desertion kept me from wanting to involve myself in something new and different. Oh, well, I'll give it a try.

Your daughter, Berkeley

P.S. Will we always be relative strangers? Only time will tell.

Fine, Anne. **Flour Babies.** Little, Brown, 1992, 178pp. Grades 6-8. A Carnegie Medal winner.

Realistic fiction. *Peer pressure; responsibility; rites of passage; school.*

Note: *Anne Fine is an excellent writer who discusses relevant topics with fascinating characters. Even the older elementary students will enjoy this one.*

"An explosion of 124 pounds of white flour? In my classroom? With that bunch of delinquents?"

When Simon heard his teacher, Mr. Cassidy, ranting and raving to Dr. Devoy, he couldn't wait to announce to the students before their teacher arrived: "Hey, those flour babies! They're going to be the best ever! At the end–a big explosion!"

That's how Room Eight–the toughest and laziest students in school–began the course in child development. The rules were simple. Flour babies will always be kept clean and dry. Flour babies will be weighed twice a week for any weight loss. Flour babies will be attended at all times.

Simon had to take his flour baby with him everywhere. What would those rough tough guys on the soccer team say?

Fine, Anne. **The Tulip Touch.** Little Brown, 1997, 149pp. Grades 6-9.

Realistic fiction. *Ethics; friendship; peer pressure; responsibility.*

 This book could be read by elementary students as well, but the issues of responsibility and peer pressure seem more appropriate for middle school students. This book is also recommended for older reluctant readers.

Natalie had only one friend–Tulip. Having only Tulip as a friend was quite enough.

Tulip had a way of making life exciting. She was a great story-teller and loved to exaggerate. Actually, she lied. That lie would carry one grain of truth to make it believable. Natalie's dad called Tulip's technique the Tulip Touch.

Tulip could be mean. Once she wrapped a present of dried dog mess and gave it to Jamie Whitton. "Merry Christmas," Tulip said sweetly.

There were all kinds of games Natalie and Tulip played: Candy Swipe, Trash Bin Fire, Exploding Greenhouse, and Wild Night. Natalie was tiring of these childish games. Natalie also knew that Tulip was capable of revenge.

How can a person gently end a friendship?

Fleischman, Paul. **Dateline: Troy.** Candlewick Press, 1996, 80pp. Grades 6 & Up.

Nonfiction. *Revenge; rivalry; war; World War I; World War II.*

 This book can be used for all ages as a comparative history tool.

How would the Trojan War be reported in the today's media? Is the Trojan War similar to other recent conflicts like the Gulf War? Are Achilles, Cassandra, and Odysseus similar to other people in recent history?

This book retells the Trojan War story by comparing it with authentic newspaper clips of modern events, from World War I to the Gulf War.

Have we as a human race changed? Read *Dateline: Troy* and decide for yourself.

Fleischman, Paul. **A Fate Totally Worse than Death.** Candlewick Press, 1995, 124pp. Grades 7 & Up.

Humor. *Revenge; rivalry; substance abuse.*

Note: *Explain before or afterwards that this book is a satire of the* **Fear Street** *series and Christopher Pike books. You might need to define the word "satire."*

Danielle drops her copy of the book *Prom Night Massacre* to glance at her reflection. Perfect, of course. Terrific legs. Classic, beach-bunny figure. Blond, straight, faultless hair. A Pepsi–ad quality face. Ambitious, selfish, materialistic. Just like the main character in *Prom Night Massacre.*

Except characters in books always pay for their sins. Not Danielle. She has already committed murder and plans to do it again.

See, there's this new girl in school, a Norwegian beauty named Helga, who has the guys gasping for breath. Danielle and her friends plan to change all that. They plan to have Helga gasping for breath – like, permanently!

Fletcher, Susan. **Flight of the Dragon Kyn.** Antheneum, 1993, 213pp. Grades 6 & Up.

Fantasy. *Animals (birds and dragons); magic; revenge; supernatural; war.*

I can call the birds as others can call dogs. Birds come to me and I can help them.

I'm Kara. I've been summoned by King Orrik to use my bird call to call down the dragons that have been plundering his kingdom.

Little did I foresee that I would become part of the fierce rivalry between King Orrick and his jealous brother, Rog. Gudjen, the king's sister, is thought to be a witch. She believes I am capable of bringing the dragons by my call.

How can I call down dragons for the king? I have never seen a dragon!

Fox, Paula. **Western Wind.** Orchard, 1993, 201pp. Grades 6 & Up.

Realistic fiction. *Aging; illness (physical); rites of passage; trust.*

At the time I didn't know that my 12th summer would be the most memorable one of my life. It started off horribly. I was sent away because of a new baby brother, whom I detested. I was sent to stay with Gran, who lives off the coast of Maine. She lived in a cottage without electricity or plumbing. What a drag!

Gran was quite a character. All she cared about was painting and poetry. She introduced me to the Herkimers, the strangest family I had ever met. They liked to think of themselves as the Cosby family when they really resembled the Simpsons.

I had no idea this summer would hold bittersweet memories that would entrap and entice me for a lifetime.

Goldman, E. M. **Getting Lincoln's Goat.** Delacorte, 1995, 215pp. An Eliot Armbruster Mystery. Grades 6-9.

Humor. *Love; peer pressure; rivalry; revenge; school; sports; work.*

Elliot decides to be a detective for his Life Skills class. For experience he tags along with a real detective, Devlin McGray. That experience almost cost Elliot some teeth!

However, Elliot is more prepared when the school's mascot—a goat–is stolen. He knows to look for the droppings, of course, and any other obvious clues. His classmates, and especially the pretty ace reporter Pam Culhane, are counting on him.

Will Elliot get his goat? Or will the mystery get Elliot's goat?

Goldman, William. **The Princess Bride: S. Morgenstern's Classic Tale of True Love and High Adventure.** Ballantine, 1993, 283pp. Grades 6 & Up.

Folklore. *Love; magic; movie novels; revenge; rivalry.*

Note: Screenwriter William Goldman has adapted this book from a novel he loved as a boy. He has edited out the "boring" chapters and retained the fast pace. This tale is a good companion to Robin McKinley's **Beauty** and **Rose Daughter**, as well as other fractured fairy tales. Some middle school students have said this is their favorite book.

Long ago, there lived a beautiful girl named Buttercup. She was engaged to marry Prince Humperdinck. Then she was known throughout the land as the Princess Bride.

Princess Buttercup did not love her Prince, nor did he love her. The Prince loved only himself and hunting. The Prince owned a Zoo of Death that was kept brimming with animals he could hunt and kill.

Princess Buttercup had once given her heart to a farm boy named Wesley, who was presumed dead. The Princess vowed to love no other. The day before the wedding the Princess Bride was kidnapped by three bloodthirsty varmints.

Fencing. Fighting. Torture. True love. Hate. Revenge. Chases. Escapes. Passion. Pain. Death.

All of these emotions and adventures are in *The Princess Bride*. Read it. Enjoy.

Grant, Cynthia D. **Keep Laughing.** Atheneum, 1991, 164pp. Grades 6 & Up.

Realistic fiction. *Problem parents; self-identity; show business; trust.*

Hello, everybody. Welcome to my comedy act. I know you're thinking that at 15, I know nothing about comedy. Wrong, wrong, wrong. You see, my childhood was one big joke. One continual yuk after another. My childhood—yuk!

Maybe you've heard of my father, the comedian Joey Young. You've probably seen him on the tube. That's where I usually see him. In fact, until I was 10, I thought he was six inches tall! Yuk, yuk, yuk.

Maybe you think comedians are funny off the tube, away from the spotlight. Not true. Comedians are sad people. My dad and I are the saddest people around. We just keep laughing to keep from crying. We keep you laughing so you won't spot our tears.

As I leave, I want you to remember: no matter what happens, keep laughing.

Grant, Cynthia D. **Shadow Man.** Macmillan, 1992, 149pp. Grades 7 & Up. An ALA Best Books for Young Adults selection.

Realistic fiction. *Death; sex and sexuality; substance abuse (alcohol).*

Note: This is a fascinating account told by many points of view. Recommend this one to teachers, as well.

Something terrible has happened. Gabriel McCloud is dead; he smashed his truck into a tree. Drunk, of course. Now he is just a shadow, a memory.

Somehow the memories of Gabe are not so easy to forget. Everyone in town liked him, from his favorite teacher, Carolyn Sanders, to his pregnant girlfriend, Jennie Harding. Even the mortician's son, Don Morrison, remembers him fondly.

Now Gabe will be the Shadow Man in their lives. He has been terminated, just like his favorite comic book character Shadow Man.

No one will ever be the same again.

Grant, Cynthia D. **Uncle Vampire.** Atheneum, 1993. Grades 7 & Up. An ALA Best Books for Young Adults selection.

Realistic fiction. *Eating disorders; problem parents; secrets; sexual abuse; substance abuse (alcohol); trust.*

 Note: *This book uses vampirism as an analogy of sexual abuse. Some teenagers read the book as a literal book about vampires. There's a surprise ending, too, which is believable.*

Secrets. So many secrets are hidden and never discussed. Consider the dark secret that Uncle Vampire comes at night and drains you of all your blood and energy. Uncle Vampire can even turn you into a vampire. The only way to destroy a vampire is to bring the vampire into the light.

Carolyn and her twin sister, Honey, know that their uncle is a vampire. Carolyn wants to tell someone about the nights that Uncle Vampire sneaks into their room to drink their blood.

Whom can she tell? She's only 16. Her parents have their problems. Her older sister Maggie is away at college. Her brother is having a nervous breakdown.

Whom can Carolyn tell about her Uncle Vampire without being called crazy?

Greene, Patricia Baird. **The Sabbath Garden.** Lodestar/Dutton, 1993, 214pp. Grades 6-9. An ALA Best Books for Young Adults selection.

Realistic fiction. *African Americans; death; Jews; interracial relations; responsibility; sexual abuse; substance abuse (alcohol).*

 Note: *This book subtly discusses the reasons for graffiti in crowded cities and why it provides an outlet for Opie's frustrations.*

Wildcat!

Opie thinks of herself as a wildcat longing to escape her crowded and cramped life. She lives in a dilapidated apartment building on Manhattan's Lower East Side.

One day she buys some spray paint and sprays "WILDCAT" on her building. That action leads to her friendship with Solomon Leshko, an elderly tenant. What can an African-American teenager and an elderly Jewish man possibly have in common? As it turns out, they both share something that fulfills all their hopes and dreams: the Sabbath garden.

Griffin, Penni R. **Switching Well.** Margaret K. McElderry Books, 1993, 218pp. Grades 7-9.

Fantasy. *Time travel; women's issues.*

Would you like to travel through time? Wait. Don't answer until you've read this book.

Ada wishes to live "a hundred years from now," when women would be treated equally. When Ada time travels to the 1990s, she is shocked by the drug pushers, child molesters, and homeless shelters. Oh, yes, and just what are immunizations, anyway?

Amber longs to travel backward in time, when parents stayed together instead of divorcing. When Amber travels back to the 1890s, she is shocked. There is harsh discipline by adults, dull routines of chores, and a lack of privacy. Oh, yes, and taking one bath a week is just plain disgusting!

It doesn't take much time for both girls to long for the good old days. Can they cross time and space to return home?

Guy, Rosa. **The Friends.** Holt, Rinehart & Winston, 1973, 185pp. Grades 6 & Up.

Realistic fiction. *African Americans; friendship; interracial relations; sexual abuse.*

Note: Edith's father has sexually molested and abused his family, but it is subtly discussed. However, this could be disturbing to some readers.

I never wanted to be friends with Edith. She was always late to class. She always looked a mess, with big holes in her socks. She just wasn't my type of friend.

Besides, I had my problems with my crazy dad and those hateful kids at school making fun of my Trinidad accent.

Even with Edith as my friend, I was always wary of her. She just didn't look right.

When I lost Edith's friendship, I didn't know how badly I would hurt Edith and her family. I didn't know what harm I would cause. I wish I could change my rude behavior toward her. I wish more than anything we could be as we used to be–friends.

Hahn, Mary Downing. **December Stillness.** Clarion, 1988; (Pbk.) Avon, 1990, 181pp. Grades 7-9.

Realistic fiction. *Homeless; illness (mental); men's issues; suicide; Vietnam War.*

I'm "Mad Dog" McAllister, the craziest girl in Adelphia.

What makes me crazy? Well, my friends and family think I'm crazy to want to talk to Mr. Weems. Mr. Weems is a homeless Vietnam veteran who hangs out in the library. I really need his help on my research paper about the homeless. Instead, he either avoids me or tells me to leave him alone. Once he threw a magazine at me. That display resulted in my being kicked out of the public library. It also led to an accident that would haunt me for the rest of my life.

Call me crazy, but why can't Mr. Weems' name be on the Vietnam memorial? After all, he is a casualty of the war. It just took him longer to die.

Hahn, Mary Downing. **Look for Me by Moonlight.** Clarion Books, 1995, 198pp. Grades 7-9. An ALA Best Books for Young Adults selection.

Horror. *Love; occult; stepparents; supernatural; trust.*

"I've come to you by moonlight, Cynda."

Stop. I know what you're going to say. Vincent Maranthos is too old for me. He says he's at least "two or three centuries old." To me he seems about 30. Vincent is so handsome and so charming. Who cares about his age and, well, those small bites on my neck?

Besides, at 16 I'm certainly old enough to take care of myself. Nobody cares anyway. My Dad, my stepmother, and my half-brother are too engrossed with their own lives and problems.

I can handle the mysterious Vincent Maranthos by moonlight.

Or can I?

Hamilton, Virginia. **Plain City.** Blue Sky, 1993, 194pp. Grades 6 & Up.

Realistic fiction. *African Americans; homeless; illness (mental); self-identity; Vietnam War.*

Buhlaire Sims looks different from everyone else in Plain City: vanilla skin, blue hazel eyes, rasta hair. She doesn't have a regular home life, either. Her mom is the fan dancer and singer Bluezy Sims. Her dad is dead, missing in action during the Vietnam War.

At least Buhlaire thinks he's dead. Then her school principal gives her a note:

Buhlaire, the Vietnam War ended in 1975. You were born around 1980. Your dad is still alive. He lives right here in Plain City.

That very day Buhlaire begins her search for her dad. Maybe when she finds her dad, she will finally find herself.

Heneghan, James. **Torn Away.** Viking, 1994, 183pp. Grades 6 & Up.

Realistic fiction. *Crime; Ireland; revenge; runaways; war.*

At 13, Declan is a terrorist.

Born and raised in Belfast, Ireland, Declan is seeking revenge for the death of his parents and his sister. Handcuffed to the seat on a flight to Vancouver, Canada, Declan is sent to live with his Uncle Matthew and family. Declan vows to return to Ireland.

Uncle Matthew, Aunt Kate, and his cousins, Ana and Thomas, are not willing to let Declan go back to Ireland. Declan scornfully calls them "the fixers" because they think they can fix bad situations with love. To get Declan to stay with the family, Uncle Matthew reveals a terrible secret about Declan's father. That secret devastates Declan.

Will Declan be torn away from his new family just as he was torn away from Ireland?

Hesse, Karen. **Out of the Dust.** Scholastic, 1997, 227pp. Grades 6 & Up. A Newbery Award winner.

Poetry. *Death; disability; illness; work; women's issues.*

This book is a collection of free verse by the main character, a 15-year-old girl named Billie Jo. She relates the hardships of living on her family's wheat farm in Oklahoma during the 1930s. When Billie Joe's father accidentally starts a fire, Billie Jo is badly burned and her mother eventually dies. I usually choose two of the poems to introduce the style and plot of the book. "Dazzled" is about her mother's piano playing; "The Accident" describes the fire that occurs. One poem is about joy; the other, despair.

Hesse, Karen. **Phoenix Rising.**
Henry Holt, 1994, 182pp.
Grades 6 & Up.

Romance. *Death; end-of-the-world;
ecology; illness (physical); love.*

Radiation scares me the most. That is everyone's fear these days.
Before radiation, life was okay. Then the Cookshire nuclear
power plant had an accident. Now my life is filled with protective
masks, evacuations, contaminated food. And death.

My Gran's back room is the dying room. My mother and grandfather died there. Now a "refugee" family from the nuclear accident
is living there. And dying.

How can I let myself fall in love with Ezra, knowing that our love
will die when he dies?

Hinton, S. E. **Taming the Star
Runner.** Delacorte, 1988, 159pp.
Grades 6 & Up.

Realistic fiction. *Responsibility; rites of
passage; work.*

Travis Harris knows he's cool. He's got the looks, style, and
brains when he chooses to use them. He has only one major character
defect: his bad temper. His temper lands him in trouble when he
throttles his stepfather. Travis ends up being sent to his uncle's ranch
to chill out.

The trouble is that no one else thinks Travis is cool. Ignored at
the new school and at the ranch where he works, he begins to have
self-doubts. His crush on Casey Kencaide doesn't help his confidence,
either. She's at least two years older than Travis and is the riding
instructor at the ranch. She sees right through Travis, spotting the
insecure person inside. So does his uncle, who takes no nonsense or
abuse from Travis.

What's a guy to do?

Hinton, S. E. **Tex.** HarperCollins, 1979,
191pp. Grades 6 & Up.

Realistic fiction. *Men's issues; movie
novels; rites of passage; substance
abuse.*

There's two groups of people in my town: those that's staying
and those that's going.

I'm staying. Those that's staying don't have big plans and don't
plan to do nothing from day to day, year to year.

My older brother Mason is going. Those that's going have big
plans to get out of this turkey town as quick as school ends. Mason's
bound to get a scholarship, being a basketball ace and all. Me, I'll be
lucky to get through high school, what with me getting expelled for
gluing caps on the typewriter keys.

Wait, I'm getting ahead of myself here. Since I got shot, I don't
keep things in order no more.

Yeah, I got shot up. I almost got arrested for shoplifting–which I
didn't do. I dealt some drugs. That is, Les dealt drugs; I just went for
the ride. Mason and me got held hostage by a hitchhiking ex-con.
Wait, I got it all out of order again.

You'll have to read my book, *Tex*, to get it all in the right order.

Hoppe, Joanne. **Dream Spinner.**
Morrow Jr., 1992, 228pp. Grades 6-9.

Fantasy. *Death; occult; supernatural; time travel.*

After giving a book report on dreams, Mary is fascinated by the subject. She reads about dream spinner, a way to dream yourself into any time or place. That night Mary dream spins 100 years in the past, becoming acquainted with a fashionable young couple, who call her Christabel. The couple take her to fashionable balls and skating parties.

Night after night Mary dream spins to visit the past. Each time she hears an eerie train whistle. What does the whistle mean? Is Mary's presence a threat to the couple? Will Mary be locked in time, unable to return?

Hotze, Sollace. **Acquainted with the Night.** Clarion, 1992, 230pp. Grades 6-9.

Mysteries/thrillers. *Love; occult; supernatural; time travel.*

Molly never expected to fall in love, especially with a Vietnam war veteran. Caleb McLaughlin is all Molly ever dreamed about–and more.

Molly and Caleb share a secret. They have both seen the ghost of Evaline Raintree. The ghost seems to be warning them of something, but she disappears as suddenly as she appears.

What is this ghost trying to say to them? Perhaps the ghost is warning them about their romance.

You see, Mollie and Caleb are first cousins.

Hotze, Sollace. **A Circle Unbroken.**
Houghton Mifflin, 1988, 224pp.; (Pbk.)
Houghton Mifflin, 1989, 244pp.
Grades 6 & Up.

Historical fiction. *Native Americans; love; problem parents; self-identity.*

In 1838 Rachel Porter is finally going home. She has been missing for seven years. At 10 she was captured by the Sioux Indians. Now white bounty hunters have found her and have returned her to her family.

It is not an easy adjustment for Rachel. Her father forbids her to talk about her past life. Instead Rachel writes about her life as Kata Wi ("Blazing Sun" for her red hair). She tells of her life as the adopted daughter of the chief, her love for White Hawk, and, especially, her love for Sioux folklore.

Like a circle unbroken, Rachel must make peace with her two lives and blend them into a continuous symbol of identity.

Hunt, Irene. **Across Five Aprils.**
Follett, 1964, 190 pp. Grades 6 & Up.

Historical fiction. *Civil War; death; family; rites of passage.*

Note: This book is written in a slow-moving, archaic style. For the best results, this might be used as a read-aloud. A pullout map is included.

Life is hard for the Creighton family. The family is torn apart by the War Between the States. Brother Tom and cousin Eb fight for the Union. Brother Bill fights for the South and is never heard from again. Tom is killed at Shiloh. Eb deserts the Union Army and wants to return home.

Jethro Creighton matures into a man during those five Aprils. He even writes a letter to President Lincoln, explaining the situation regarding his brother who deserted. Lincoln replies, saying that if Eb returns by a certain day, there will no punishment.

Follow nine-year-old Jethro Creighton's rite of passage across five Aprils.

Jackson, Livia Bitton. **I Have Lived a Thousand Years: Growing Up in the Holocaust.** Simon & Schuster for Young People, 1997, 224pp. Grades 7 & Up. An ALA Best Books for Young Adults selection.

Biography. *Europe (Hungary); Holocaust; Jews; religious prejudice; World War II.*

In Hungary in 1944, my family and I were forced to wear yellow stars. I called the star the Jew badge.

I refused to leave the house wearing that ugly yellow star. It was just too humiliating. However, my brother cut a star out of cardboard, and covered it with glistening golden-yellow silk fabric. It looked like a military medal. He wore it proudly. It was the envy of all his friends.

Years later I would laugh bitterly at that small humiliation. My family would eventually be separated, tortured, and killed just for being Jews. I was only 13 at the time, but I had already lived a thousand years. Let me share my story with you.

Johnston, Julie. **Hero of Lesser Causes.** Little, Brown, 1993, 194pp. Grades 6 & Up. An ALA Best Books for Young Adults selection.

Realistic fiction. *Disability (physical); illness (physical); self-identity.*

I love a dare. So does my older brother, Patrick. That is, he used to love a dare. One horrible day we dared each other to wade in a disgusting, leech-infested pond. We had no idea that Patrick would contract polio and become paralyzed.

The doctor said Patrick's first year is the "telling year," the year when the most progress would be made. Patrick just lies in bed. Sometimes he screams obscenities at us or says he wishes he were dead.

How can I help Patrick take on the most important dare of his life—the dare to fight for his health and for his life?

Jones, Diana Wynne. **Howl's Moving Castle.** Greenwillow, 1986, 212pp. Grades 6 & Up.

Fantasy. *Love; magic; occult; supernatural.*

Everyone is frightened when a black castle appears on the horizon in the land of Ingary. They learn the castle belongs to Wizard Howl, who, it is said, likes to suck the souls of young girls.

Until the castle appears, the Hatter sisters think they are quite normal. Suddenly Lettie and Martha switch identities, and Sophie is transformed into an ugly old hag by the Witch of the Waste. Sophie decides to venture into Howl's castle to see if he will reverse the spell.

Sophie finds out her problem is minimal compared to the strange happenings at Howl's Moving Castle. First, there's the demon fire, whose face appears within the flames. Then there's the dog, who changes into a man from time to time. Of course, there's Howl, who is always falling in love with fair maidens. Apparently, these creatures are all under some sort of spell, too.

The thing to do is to break the spell, but it's hard to get these creatures to agree to anything. In this humorous fantasy nothing is what it seems and everything is backward in Howl's moving castle.

Jordan, Sherryl. **Winter of Fire.**
Scholastic, 1992, 321pp.
Grades 6 & Up.

Fantasy. *Abuse; love; magic; occult; rivalry; supernatural; women's issues.*

I am Elsha, born in a world of fire and darkness, a child of the Quelled. The Quelled are people predestined to serve the ruling class, the Chosen. We Quelled wear brands on our forehead to distinguish us from the rulers. I have never forgotten the agony, the shock, and the outrage of being blindfolded and branded. Perhaps this anger has served me well. I have too much pride to believe that I am inferior to the Chosen.

My pride leads me to being condemned to death on my 16th birthday. Luckily, the Firelord saves me and selects me to be his Handmaiden. I am the first Quelled female to be so honored. The Firelord is the most powerful being on earth because his powers lead us to the coal so vital to our dark and cold world.

When the Firelord dies, I am heir to his position. My challenger, Zune, vows to raise an army of the Chosen to fight me until death. Although I am not a violent person, I will never relinquish my powers until the Quelled have the justice and freedom denied them for thousands of years.

If freedom requires a revolution, I am ready!

Keehn, Sally M.. **I Am Regina.**
Philomel, 1991, 240pp. Grades 8 & Up.

Historical fiction. *Abuse; Native Americans; sexual abuse.*

Note: This book can be harsh in its portrayal of life. For example, although the author portrays the abuse subtly, Regina is raped by her adopted father.

A tombstone stands in Christ's Church cemetery near present-day Stouchsburg, Pennsylvania. The inscription reads:

> *REGINA LEININGER*
> *In Legend Regina Hartman*
> *As a small child held Indian captive 1755-1763*
> *Identified by her mother's singing the hymn*
> *"Alone, Yet Not Alone Am I"*

What happened to Regina during those lost years as an Indian captive? How was she treated? How did the soldiers find her? Based on a true story, this book tells the story of Regina's lost years after her family are either separated or killed.

Kindl, Patrice. **Owl in Love.** Houghton Mifflin, 1993, 204pp. Grades 6 & Up. An ALA Best Books for Young Adults selection.

Romance. *Animals (owls); love; occult; secrets; supernatural.*

I am in love with Mr. Lindstrom, my science teacher. Every night I fly to his window and watch him sleep. He sleeps in his underwear. Fruit of the Loom, size 34.

I am Owl. It is my name as well as my nature. At night I am Owl. During the day I am an ordinary girl attending the local high school.

Then I meet Houle, a creature like myself, part Owl and human. Whom will I choose—Mr. Lindstrom or Houle?

It's so difficult to be an owl in love!

Koertge, Ron. **The Harmony Arms.** Little, Brown, 1992, 137pp. Grades 6 & Up.

Realistic fiction. *Homosexuality; problem parents; show business; single parents.*

The Harmony Arms is the weirdest apartment house in Los Angeles. You don't have to be crazy to live there, but it helps.

Gabriel is pretty sane for a teenager, but his puppeteer dad always talks through his puppet, Timmy. Gabriel's best friend, Tess, always carries a video camera because she's filming her life story and calling it *Mondo Tess.* Tess's mother, Mona, is a struggling actress who plays aspirin tablets and giant ants in TV commercials

Get the picture? You don't have to be crazy to enjoy this book, but it helps. (So does a sense of humor!)

Koller, Jackie French. **The Primrose Way.** Harcourt Brace, 1992, 275pp. With glossary, bibliography, pronunciation guide. Grades 6 & Up.

Historical fiction. *Love; Native Americans; interracial relations.*

 Note: *I highly recommend this love story, which is authentic in its presentation of Native American culture and includes bibliographic references and a pronunciation guide.*

In 1663 Rebekah joins her missionary father in a newly established Puritan settlement in the New World. Only 16, she first regards the Pawtucket tribe of Indians as savages. She's shocked by their uncovered bodies and their strange customs. However, once she gets to know Qunnequawese (Young Doe) and learns the language, she begins to wonder just how "uncivilized" these unusual creatures are.

Rebekah is fascinated by Mishannock (Daybreak Star). Could this medicine man be practicing black magic? What kind of man would be raised by wolves? What kind of man would pretend not to understand the Mother's English?

Could it be that Rebekah is falling in love with this mysterious medicine man?

Krisher, Trudy. **Spite Fences.** Delacorte, 1994, 283pp. Grades 6 & Up.

Historical fiction. *African Americans; crime; racism; responsibility; secrets; trust.*

 Note: *This book could be used as a read-aloud for all ages. The author attempts to be authentic to the Sixties, even including the use of period-specific slang and dialect.*

Maggie Pugh knew a terrible secret. She was an eyewitness to a horrific event.

Many unusual events were happening in the South during the Sixties. This decade was the time the Civil Rights Movement fiercely combated harsh racism. In Kinship, Georgia, people were identified by their race and income. You were either rich or poor, white or "colored." Maggie was poor and colored.

Maggie had talent and persistence. She was a natural photographer and a hard worker. She also cleaned George Hardy's house to earn money.

Maggie had never met anyone like this Northerner George Hardy. He considered himself "black," not "colored." He supported the Civil Rights Movement. He had opinions that she had never heard before.

Maggie decided that she could trust only George Hardy with her haunting secret.

Klass, David. **California Blue.**
Scholastic Hardcover, 1994, 200pp.
Grades 7-9.

Realistic fiction. *Ecology; ethics; illness
(physical); problem parents;
responsibility; rivalry; science; sports
(track and field).*

I like to run and I like to collect butterflies. Sometimes I take my net with me while I'm running through a redwood forest. I never dreamed that catching a butterfly in the redwood forest would lead to such a scandal in our mill town. That butterfly turned out to be a missing link in the evolution of butterflies and moths. That didn't set too well with the workers in the local lumber mill. They don't want to stop progress over some stupid butterfly.

I never dreamed that my dad and I would take opposite sides on this issue. Of course, he does work for the lumber mill, so it's just another thing to keep us apart. We're not close, my dad and I. Everyone says he's the perfect father, so I guess it's my fault. All my older brothers and sisters have turned out exactly the way he wanted: two cheerleaders and two high school football stars.

Now I find out my dad has leukemia and I've created a town scandal. How can I get myself out of this mess?

Konigsburg, E. L. **T-Backs, T-Shirts, Coat and Suit.** Atheneum, 1993, 165pp. Grades 6 & Up.

Realistic fiction. *Work; women's issues.*

 This book discusses women's issues in an amusing way.

A *T-back* is a two-piece bathing suit. The bottom half when seen from the rear, forms a T. A T-shirt—well, you know what *that* is. *Coat* stands for "Citizens Opposing All T-Backs." A suit is a lawsuit against *Coat.*

Got all that? No? Then you better read this hilarious account of what happens when two ladies wear T-backs to sell food to shipyard and dock workers.

Krull, Kathleen. **Lives of the Writers: Comedies, Tragedies (and What the Neighbors Thought).** Illustrated by the author. Harcourt Brace, 1994, 95pp. Grades 6 & Up. Part of a series, including: **Lives of the Musicians: Good Times, Bad Times (and What the Neighbors Thought); Lives of the Artists: Masterpieces, Messes (and What the Neighbors Thought);** and **Lives of the Athletes: Thrills, Spills (and What the Neighbors Thought).**

Biography. *Interracial relations; secrets; substance abuse; war.*

 This is an excellent series for reluctant readers who think they don't like biographies.

I'll bet you didn't know that Edgar Allen Poe was a habitual liar. He even lied about his wife's death. He said her poor health was due to a singing accident when she broke a blood vessel and coughed up blood. Instead, his wife died of tuberculosis. He married his wife when she was 13. They were first cousins. His life really kept the neighbors gossiping.

I'll bet you didn't know the gossip about Miquel de Cervantes. He was the Spanish author of *Don Quixote of La Mancha.* The author fought a duel, lost his left hand in a war, was kidnapped by pirates, and was held for ransom for five years.

I'll bet you didn't know Shakespeare was a well-respected actor who played the "ghost" in *Hamlet.*

I'll bet you didn't know . . .

Never mind. I'll bet you'll enjoy the gossip in the *Lives of the Writers: Comedies, Tragedies (and what the Neighbors Thought).*

Laird, Elizabeth. **Kiss the Dust.**
Dutton, 1992, 284pp.; (Pbk.) Puffin,
1994, 288pp. Grades 6 & Up.

Historical fiction. *Homeless; immigrants;
Middle East; religion; religious prejudice;
war.*

 Note: The book offers detailed information about the Kurds in the epilogue.

Tara lives an idyllic life in Iraq until she witnesses the shooting of a young boy by soldiers. She realizes that being a Kurd in Iraq during the Iran-Iraq war is dangerous. Her family flees to Iran, through the Zagros mountains, to find freedom.

However, there is no freedom in Iran, either. The Kurds number more than 20 million people, but they have no country of their own. The Iranians mock the Kurds' custom of wearing bright clothes. Sometimes the Kurds are sent to concentration camps with deplorable conditions.

Tara's family has no choice but to flee to London. Now Tara must adjust to the free attitude and dress of the British people.

When will Tara ever find a home where she is accepted?

Lasky, Kathryn. **Memoirs of a Bookbat.** Harcourt, Brace, 1994, 215pp. Grades 6 & Up.

Realistic fiction. *Diaries; problem parents; religion; secrets; self-identity.*

Don't call me a bookworm. I love books, but there's nothing wormy about it. I would rather be called a bat than a worm any day of the week.

Books are my friends. I have never been in one school long enough to do a whole term project, let alone make a friend. Every new classroom was different, but I could always count on a library to be familiar.

My family calls themselves migrants for God. My parents are born-again Christians who like to see everyone from the same viewpoint. Me, I don't know what I think. I know I don't like their friend, Nettie, telling me what is acceptable reading. She believes in banning the stories *Brer Rabbit* and *Goldilocks*. I mean, come on!

I'm great at living two lives, though. I live one as a goody-goody. I live the other as a sneaky reader. I hide all my banned books in a secret compartment on our super-deluxe Roadmaster trailer.

How long can I pull off this deception?

Lee, Marie. **Finding My Voice.**
Houghton Mifflin, 1992, 165pp. Grades
6 & Up. First in a series: **Saying
Goodbye** follows.

Realistic fiction. *Asian Americans;
interracial relations; love; problem
parents; racism; self-identity.*

I'm Ellen Sung, the only Asian American in a small school in Minnesota. I'm having trouble finding my voice.

Who am I? Am I destined to follow my sister to Harvard simply because my parents think I should? Will I receive my letter in gymnastics? Should I date Tomper, a boy I've had a crush on for years? Most importantly, can I learn to forgive the racial comments that I hear on the school bus, at school events, or even on my graduation night?

Maybe when I find my voice I will find my identity.

LeMieux, A. C. **The TV Guidance Counselor.** Tambourine/William Morris, 1993, 137pp. Grades 7 & Up.

Realistic fiction. *Divorce; illness (mental); responsibility; suicide.*

I don't think I was trying to kill myself the night I jumped into the Mohegan River. My shrink keeps asking me question after question, but I just don't feel like answering them. Things like how I feel about my parents' divorce. How does he think I feel? Great?

I wonder if I'm as crazy as that loony tune we call the TV Guidance Counselor. This guy used to come to the grocery store to flip through all the *TV Guide* magazines without buying. Maybe in some strange way I'm like that nut. Maybe I'm afraid of buying into life so I'd rather just snap pictures with my camera and not get involved.

I guess I wasn't trying to kill myself when I jumped into the river. I was just trying to wash away the pain. I can't stand any more pain.

Maybe when I tell you my story, you'll understand.

Lester, Julius. **Othello: A Novel.** Scholastic Hardcover, 1995, 151pp. Grades 6 & Up. An ALA Best Books for Young Adults selection.

Historical fiction. *Crime; death; ethics; interracial relations; love; racism; rivalry; suicide; trust.*

Do me a favor on this novel. Forget Shakespeare and all that you think he represents, will you? Just enjoy this ageless tale about love, trust, and betrayal.

Maybe it would surprise you to know that William Shakespeare wrote plays for uneducated audiences and not for scholars. In his time Shakespeare was considered to be quite bawdy, and he always had a great story to tell. Usually he borrowed the story from a novel and then worked out the characterizations with his brand of genius.

Take Othello, for instance. Shakespeare lifted the plot from an Italian novel. The story concerns a black African who marries a white beauty only to murder her when he suspects her of infidelity. Othello's tragic suspicions are planted by his best friend, Iago.

Lester has updated most of the Elizabethan English, but he keeps the compelling plot. Some interesting changes: Iago is an African and the setting is in England.

Perhaps you'll find the tale of Othello is one love story that never grows old.

Levine, Gail Carson. **Ella Enchanted.**
HarperCollins, 1997, 232pp.; (Pbk.)
HarperTrophy, 1998, 232pp. Grades 6 &
Up. A Newbery Honor book; an ALA Best
Books for Young Adults selection.

Folklore. *Love; magic; Middle Ages;
supernatural; women's issues.*

 Note: *This Cinderella retelling
is really for all ages. Use
this book with Robin
McKinley's* **Beauty: The Retelling
of Beauty and the Beast,** *Diane
Curtis Regon's* **Princess
Nevermore,** *William Goldman's*
The Princess Bride, *Patricia
Wrede's dragon series, and Bruce
Coville's* **The Dragonslayers.** *All
are fractured fairy tales.*

At my christening I was given the gift of obedience by the
fairy Lucinda. That gift turned out the be a curse. Anyone could
command me and I would do it. It had to be a direct command,
such as "hop on one foot." A wish or request had no effect. "Why
don't you go to bed?" could be ignored. If you commanded me to
cut off my head, I would have to do it. I was in danger every
moment.

Now that my two stepsisters, Hattie and Olive, know of my
curse, they order me around like Cinderella.

So what am I to do? Am I to remain Ella enchanted?

Levitin, Sonia. **Annie's Promise.**
Atheneum, 1993, 186pp. Grades 6-8.

Realistic fiction. *Jews; interracial
relations; religious prejudice; revenge;
rivalry; sexual abuse.*

Camp is great for 13-year-old Annie, with swimming, hiking,
and riding horses. She even finds romance.

The only problem is another camper, Nancy Rae.

Nancy challenges Annie to a swimming contest, and Annie
almost drowns.

After that incident, Annie is out for revenge. Annie produces
and directs the cabin's play for the whole camp. Maybe the play is
the perfect opportunity to humiliate Nancy, the way Nancy humiliated Annie, in front of crowds of people. Yes, the play is the thing
that will give Annie her sweet revenge.

Levitin, Sonia. **The Mark of Conte.**
Macmillan, 1987, 240pp.
Grades 6 & Up.

Humor. *Computers; school.*

All you computer geeks, listen up. All the rest of you will also
appreciate this humorous book.

Conte Mark's family has just moved to California. He hates it.
His parents don't seem to mind, but they don't have to go to Vista
Mar High School, which is practically run by a computer.

For instance, the computer has Conte listed two ways: Conte
Mark and Mark Conte. This is quite a problem until Conte comes
up with a master plan that will allow him to graduate in two years
instead of four. Of course, Conte needs some help from some willing students who are eager to show off their computer skills.

Find out if Mark Conte—I mean, Conte Mark—beats the computer in *The Mark of Conte.*

Lowry, Lois. **The Giver.** Houghton Mifflin 1993, 180pp. Grades 6 & Up. A Newbery Award winner.

Fantasy. *Aging; ethics; responsibility.*

Welcome to the ideal world: a world without conflict, poverty, unemployment, injustice, or inequality.

Welcome to the annual Ceremony of Twelves. Each 12-year-old receives a life assignment by the elders. Jonas is selected to be the next receiver of Memory. This assignment was given to another 10 years ago, but this youngster failed miserably.

Will Jonas also fail at this awesome task? He meets The Giver, an elderly man who gives Jonas his memories of the past. Jonas learns about things like snow and sunshine before Climate Control. He learns about colors before Sameness controlled the mind. Most importantly, Jonas learns about love.

Which way of life is better? The old way has pain, for certain. Yet a life without pain holds no joy. Read *The Giver*, then decide.

Lowry, Lois. **A Summer to Die.** Illustrated by Jenni Oliver. Bantam Doubleday Books for Young Readers, 1977, 120pp. Grades 6 & Up.

Realistic fiction. *Death; illness (physical); rivalry; sex and sexuality.*

It was Molly who drew the line.

She drew it with chalk down our bedroom and announced, "There. Be a slob on your side of the room. My side will stay clean."

Molly and I are so different. She is neat; I am a slob. She is beautiful; I am not. She is a cheerleader; I am a photographer. She is deadly ill with leukemia; I am healthy as a horse.

Now our differences are not important. She's my sister. That's all that matters.

Lynch, Chris. **Shadow Boxer.** HarperCollins, 1992, 213pp. Grades 6-9. An ALA Best Books for Young Adults selection.

Realistic fiction. *Responsibility; rivalry; sports.*

Try this knockout of a novel that seems to be about boxing, but isn't. Sure, it has plenty of action and many fights, but most of the fights occur between brothers.

George, the older brother, is responsible for the safety and care of his younger brother, Mounty, especially since their heavy-weight boxer father died five years ago. George has to apply a knee slammer or headlock to Mounty from time to time just to keep him in line. Hey, that's what brothers are for, right?

Expect a book about boxing, but be prepared for some unexpected uppercuts by author Chris Lynch. *Shadow Boxer* will knock you out!

Lynch, Chris. **Slot Machine.** HarperCollins, 1995, 241pp. Grades 6-9. An ALA Best Books for Young Adults selection.

Realistic fiction. *Men's issues; peer pressure; revenge; self-identity; sports.*

Slotting.

That's what the camp counselors and teachers of Christian Brothers Academy call it. "We believe each man has a slot. Each man has a place in the big scheme of things. It is in everyone's best interest to find that slot at the best possible time." That's Brother Jackson's philosophy. He's the Dean of Men.

The trouble is that Elvin can't find his slot. He's too overweight and unmotivated. His best friends, Mikie and Frankie, try to help, but it's hopeless. Elvin can't play football or basketball. Swimming is a wash-out.

Hey, what about wrestling?

McDonald, Joyce. **Swallowing Stones.** Delacorte, 1997, 245pp.; (Pbk.) Dell, 1999, 245pp. Grades 7 & Up. An ALA Best Books for Young Adults selection.

Realistic fiction. *Crime; death; ethics; men's issues; responsibility; secrets.*

 Note: This book also describes the reactions of the victim's family. Everyone goes through guilt and denial. Don't miss this unforgettable book.

A bizarre death occurred on the Fourth of July in Briarwood, New Jersey. A man named Charlie Ward had been repairing shingles on his roof around noon when a bullet from nowhere dropped from the sky. He was killed instantly. The radio announcer continued on with other news of the day.

Joe spoke first. "It could have come from anywhere. It could have been anyone."

Michael MacKenzie shook his head. Who was he kidding? The announcer said it happened at noon. That was when Michael was showing off his birthday present to Joe. Michael shot his Winchester rifle in the air. The bullet wasn't supposed to go anyplace.

Michael had murdered a man. Sure, it was an accident. However, someone was dead because of his carelessness.

What should Michael do?

Magorian, Michelle. **Good Night, Mr. Tom.** HarperCollins, 1982, 366pp.; (Pbk.) HarperCollins, 1986, 366pp. Grades 6 & Up. A Carnegie Award winner.

Historical fiction. *Abuse; Great Britain; movie novels; responsibility; World War II.*

 Note: This book is a favorite of mine. Recommend it to adults, as well.

Eight-year-old Willie Beech knows that he is a bad boy. His mum says she is kinder to him than most mums are. She only gives him soft beatings. Now his mum has sent him away. It is 1940, and England has declared war on Nazi Germany. All children are evacuated to the countryside. Many families take children into their homes to keep them safe until the bombings end.

Willie is sent to live with Mr. Tom, a crusty old man. At first Willie is terrified of Mr. Tom. Gradually he learns to trust this man who doesn't believe Willie is bad or deserves beatings.

Eventually it becomes safe to return to London, but is it safe for Willie to return to his mother? Mr. Tom must send Willie back, but he tries to keep in close contact with Willie. When Willie doesn't answer his letters, Mr. Tom goes to London to find Willie.

Where is Willie? Can Mr. Tom find him before it's too late?

Marsden, John. **Letters from Inside.** Houghton Mifflin, 1991, 146pp. Grades 6 & Up.

Realistic fiction. *Abuse; crime; friendship; problem parents; secrets; trust.*

Dear Tracey,
I'm not into pen pals, but I'm bored. So I'm answering your ad. Write back.
Mandy

Dear Mandy,
Thanks for writing. Your letter was the only good answer I got. You're a good writer. I just put the ad in for a joke. Write back.
Tracey

Dear Tracey,
Now that I've been writing you for months, I can't help but notice that what you say about yourself doesn't fit. I had a friend go to your high school and he says you're not enrolled at Prescott High. I'm no Sherlock Holmes, but something smells. First you said your parents were married for 25 years, then you said your Dad died when you were born. I don't get it. Please write back . . .
Mandy

Dear Mandy,
OK, wise guy, you asked for it. If you want to keep snooping around my life, I'll tell you the truth. I'm in Garrett, a maximum security place, locked up for being bad. Now get out of my life!
Tracey

Martin, Ann M.. **Just a Summer Romance.** (Pbk.) Scholastic, 1987, 163pp. Grades 6 & Up.

Romance. *Love; show business.*

It was love at first sight.
When my Frisbee hit Justin Hart in the face, I also felt zapped, like I was hit by Cupid's arrow. It took some days of following Justin before I got his attention. I was staring at him through binoculars. He dashed over to yell at me for spying on him. Oh well, it worked. We became an item.
Justin says our love is just a summer romance and that we should never see each other again when the summer ends.
How did I know I would see his face on *People Magazine* and *TV Guide* as the newest teen idol? How can I possibly forget that?

Matas, Carol & Perry Nodelman. **Of Two Minds.** Simon & Schuster, 1995, 199pp. Grades 6 & Up. First in a series: **More Minds** follow.

Fantasy. *Magic; occult; revenge; supernatural.*

 Another twisted fairy tale for your pleasure.

It is hate at first sight.
Princess Lenora of Gepeth and Prince Coren of Andilla are expected to marry. Their parents have arranged it.
They are one strange couple. Lenora can make whatever she imagines real. Coren can read thoughts. Somehow, before the wedding ceremony, they become trapped in a world ruled by the fierce tyrant Hevak. And Hevak will never let them out of Farren Place alive.
Wait a minute. What if Coren uses his power of mind reading and Lenora uses her imagination? Would they be able to escape this horror?
Yes, it might work–if they are of two minds.

Mahy, Margaret. **The Changeover: A Supernatural Romance.** Penguin Books, 1984, 214pp. Grades 8 & Up.

Romance. *Love; magic; occult; self-identity; supernatural.*

Should she or shouldn't she?

Change over, that is, from a human being to a powerful witch, from a child to an adult.

What choice does Laura Chant have? Her brother, Jacko, is fighting for his life. What supernatural dangers will this changeover entail?

The mysterious Sorry Carlisle promises to help Laura through the transformation. He's definitely a witch—even if he is a guy.

Looks like Laura and Sorry are headed for a supernatural romance. Watch out, the changeover could be deadly!

Mahy, Margaret. **Memory.** J. M. Dents and Sons, 1987, 234pp. Grades 6 & Up,

Realistic fiction. *Death; occult; responsibility; supernatural.*

What if you can't remember any of your memories?

Take Jonny Dart, for instance. He has trouble remembering the accident that killed his sister Janine five years ago. He should remember. He was there.

Jonny hasn't seen Bonnie Benedicta since his sister's funeral, but she was the only other witness to the accident. Now Jonny must ask Bonnie a very important question: was his sister's death an accident or murder?

Mazer, Harry. **Who is Eddie Leonard?** Delacorte, 1993, 188pp. Grades 6 & Up.

Realistic fiction. *Abuse; secrets; self-identity; trust.*

I'm not Eddie Leonard. I don't care what anybody says. I'm not Eddie Leonard.

I'm Jason Diaz. I saw his face on a poster for missing children in a post office and that's when I knew. Eddie Leonard has never been loved by his family, but Jason Diaz has always been loved and missed. Eddie Leonard is a nobody; Jason Diaz comes from a perfect family with wealth, prestige, and privilege.

So when my grandmother died, I went to my new family. Here I am! Jason Diaz! I thought I would be greeted and embraced. Instead I was asked questions, questions, and more questions:

"Who are you really? Are you really Jason? Or are you Eddie Leonard pretending to be Jason? Who is Eddie Leonard?"

I'll tell you the whole story, if you'll give me a chance.

Mazer, Norma Fox. **Silver.** (Pbk.) Avon Flare, 1989, 203pp. Grades 6 & Up.

Realistic fiction. *Class conflict; friendship; sexual abuse.*

Note: This is a favorite with some teenagers.

Silver. That's my name. To be exact, my name is Sarabeth Silver, but my new friends call me Silver.

Sometimes I can't believe this group of girls are my friends. Grant, Jennifer, Asa, and Patty are so cool. They are rich, popular, and pretty. Me, I'm okay, but certainly not rich. My mom and I live in a trailer park.

You know what I've learned? Superficial things don't bring happiness. These girls have secrets in their lives more painful than anything I've ever experienced.

McKinley, Robin. **Beauty: A Retelling of Beauty and the Beast.** HarperCollins, 1978, 256pp.; (Pbk.) HarperCollins, 1993, 256pp. Grades 6 & Up.

Folklore. *Love; magic; occult; rites of passage; secrets; supernatural; trust.*

Once upon a time there was a prosperous owner of merchant ships. He was a widower with three daughters: Grace, Hope, and Honour. One day the youngest daughter–who was spoiled and willful–said, "Father, what does the name Honour mean?"

The father explained about duty and obligation. Honour interrupted him with disgust, "Huh! I would rather be called Beauty." Thus, Beauty became her name. Unfortunately, Beauty was plain and ordinary, so unlike her beautiful sisters Grace and Hope.

One day the father lost all of his ships at sea. The family lived in poverty for many years. Grace and Hope adjusted quite well, but Beauty–still being spoiled and willful–longed for a life of beauty and elegance. She begged her father to bring back a rose from one of his trips.

As we know, the father was lost in the enchanted forest, plucked a rose, and was attacked by a monstrous Beast. The Beast was looking for a beautiful girl, and, from her name, Beauty sounded like the perfect mate.

Thus begins the most famous romance between the most unlikely couple. Try this satisfying romantic fantasy and maybe you will live happily ever after, too.

McKinley, Robin. **Rose Daughter.** Greenwillow, 1997, 306pp.; (Pbk.) Mass Market Paperback, 1998, 304pp. Grades 6 & Up. An ALA Best Books for Young Adults selection.

Folklore. *Love; magic; secrets; supernatural; women's issues.*

Once upon a time, there were three rich beautiful daughters: Lionhart, Jeweltongue and Beauty. As in the folktale *Beauty and the Beast,* Lionhart and Jeweltongue could be spoiled and willful. However, Beauty was kind and pleasant.

Beauty's hobby was tending the garden. Perhaps gardening reminded Beauty of her dead mother, who smelled like a rose. Beauty's only dissatisfaction was that at night she had nightmares of meeting a monster at the end of a long corridor.

One day the father lost all his riches. While cleaning, Beauty discovered a will that left the Rose Cottage to her father. What choice did they have? They had to move and start again.

The family tried to adjust as best as they could. Lionhart dressed as a stable boy to tend the horses. Jeweltongue became a seamstress. Beauty tried to clean and garden. Still, Beauty's nightmare continued as a warning of her future.

One spring the roses would not bloom. When the father left on a trip, he promised Beauty he would bring her a rose.

Once again, we are drawn into Robin McKinley's newest version of her favorite folktale. Again, we meet Beauty and the Beast in *Rose Daughter.*

Miklowitz, Gloria D. **Desperate Pursuit.** (Pbk.) Bantam Books, 1992, 150pp. Grades 7-9.

Realistic fiction. *Abuse; love; revenge; sexual abuse.*

Nicole knows someone is following her. Someone is spying on her. Someone is intentionally frightening her.

Nicole wonders if she is being stalked by her former boyfriend, Michael. Everyone says Michael is a nice guy. How could she even think he'd try to harm her?

Nicole knows that Michael has a darker side. He's obsessed with making Nicole his girlfriend again. How far will he carry his desperate pursuit?

Mills, Claudia. **Dinah in Love.** Macmillan, 1993, 143pp. Grades 6 & Up. Part of a series, including: **Dynamite Dinah; Dinah for President;** and **Dinah Forever.**

Romance. *Love; peer pressure; school; self-identity.*

Dinah Seabrooke is acting strangely. She's always been the Girl Who Doesn't Like Boys. She didn't even ask a boy to the sixth grade dance, even though she is the publicity chairperson. The boy she hates the most is the annoying Nick Tribble.

Nick is always embarrassing her. Once he threw an exercise bra at her head. Another time he burped during the kissing scene at an audition. Worst of all, he keeps calling her Ocean-River instead of Seabrooke. Nick Tribble is the perfect excuse to hate boys forever!

Then something strange comes over Dinah. She decides to go to the dance after all. Now she desperately needs a date. All the boys she asks, like Todd and Jason, have other plans. Her best friend, Suzanne, swears that horrible Nick likes Dinah and that she should ask him to the dance.

Should Dinah risk losing her reputation as Dinah Seabrooke, Spinster Girl?

Myers, Walter Dean. **Darnell Rock Reporting.** (Pbk.) Bantam Doubleday Dell Books for Young Readers, 1994, 135pp. Grades 6 & Up.

Realistic fiction. *African Americans; homeless; politics; Vietnam War.*

Darnell Rock spends so much time in the principal's office that he was the natural choice to interview the principal. After the interview, he told the editor the article should be titled "Boring, Boring, Boring."

Then Darnell writes an article about the homeless people he saw hanging around Jackson Avenue. Darnell's editorial is spotted by members of City Council. Suddenly Darnell is a minor celebrity.

Hey, this writing business sure beats hanging around the principal's office!

Myers, Walter Dean. **The Mouse Rap.** (Pbk.) Scholastic, 1992. Grades 6-9.

Humor. *African Americans; crime; friendship; men's issues; problem parents.*

I'm not that big a dude. Five foot three and three-quarters, exactly. That's why I be called Mouse.

Me, I can hoop. I can definitely hoop. I ain't jamming, but I'm scamming. You may look great, but you will look late. I played one on one with my shadow and my shadow couldn't keep up.

But that's about all I can do. Mr. D—that's my dad who disappeared for eight years—says I should do more than just shoot hoops.

So me and the gang plan to find that treasure that Tiger Moran left. He was this criminal, see, and was supposed to have left lots of bucks.

Check out *The Mouse Rap* and see how we keep things lean and clean.

Nelson, Theresa. **The Beggar's Ride.** Orchard Books, 1992, 156pp. Grades 6 & Up.

Realistic fiction. *Homeless; runaways; survival.*

"If wishes were horses, beggars would ride."

This nursery rhyme would haunt Clare Caldwell throughout her ordeal as a homeless teenager in Atlantic City, New Jersey. Clare's main wish is to escape from "the beggar's ride" of hunger and poverty.

Clare comes across other beggars like herself. She meets Cowboy, Thimble, Shoe, Dog, and Racer. Of course, these aren't their real names. These homeless teenagers borrow names from the game *Monopoly*. For acceptance, Clare assumes the name Hat.

All these beggars are playing the game, hoping to land on Boardwalk and hit the jackpot.

Pass go and treat yourself to *The Beggar's Ride.*

O'Brien, Robert C. **Z For Zachariah.** Aladdin, 1974, 249pp. Grades 6 & Up.

Science fiction. *End-of-the-world; revenge; rivalry; science; survival.*

After the nuclear blast and radiation seepage, I am certain I am the only person left alive.

That's why I'm writing this down. I need someone to talk to, even if it's just to myself.

I am wrong. I'm not alone. Someone else is still alive. A man named John Looms is also alive. He is a scientist who wears a "safe suit" to protect him from radiation. After we meet, he takes control immediately. He becomes crazier and crazier. He reminds me of a "mad scientist" from the scary movies that I used to watch so long ago.

Now that I've survived the nuclear blast, can I survive this mad scientist?

Orlevi, Uri. **The Man from the Other Side.** English translation by Hillel Hallan. Houghton Mifflin, 1991, 186pp. Grades 6 & Up.

Historical fiction. *Europe (Poland); Jews; religious prejudice; secrets; stepparents; World War II.*

This really happened to me during World War II in Warsaw, Poland. I was 14 then. I helped my stepfather smuggle Jews through the dark, damp sewers to safety. We only did it for the money it provided us. My stepfather hated Jews, just as he hated the Germans and Communists.

My real dad was a Communist. He died in prison when I was three years old. My mom married Anthony two years later. Anthony wants to adopt me, but I won't consider it. There is no way that he can replace my father.

One day my mom tells me a secret about my dad that changes me forever. That secret results in my participation in the Warsaw Ghetto uprising, the revolt of the Jews against the Nazis.

My mom tells me my father was a Jew.

Orr, Wendy. **Peeling the Onion.** Holiday House, 1997, 166pp.; (Pbk.) Laureleaf, 1999, 166pp. Grades 7 & Up. An ALA Best Books for Young Adults selection.

Realistic fiction. *Disability (physical); rites of passage; self-identity.*

Before the accident Anna Duncan knew she was pretty, popular, and a karate expert.

After the accident Anna is confused about her place in the world. A broken neck will change her life permanently. What happens to school? What happens to her relationship with Hayden who was driving the car? What becomes of her friends? How will her family deal with her disability?

Now Anna must strip away all her layers to reveal her character. Now she must face who she really is and who she wants to become. She must begin peeling the onion.

Paterson, Katherine. **The Great Gilly Hopkins.** Avon, 1978, 148pp. Grades 5-8. A Newbery Honor book; a Young Readers' Choice Award winner.

Realistic fiction. *Adoption; disability (mental); interracial relations; responsibility; trust.*

 This book can be read by younger students, but it contains some profanity.

I am not nice. I am brilliant. I am famous across this entire country. No one wants to tangle with the great Gilly Hopkins. I am too clever and too hard to manage. Gruesome Gilly, they call me.

Ready or not, here I come. I'm going to a brand-new foster home. Miss Ellis says the lady of the house is a "nice person."

Give me a break. I eat nice people for breakfast! So, look out, Mrs. Trotter, William Ernest, and anyone else who gets in my way.

I have arrived, the great Gilly Hopkins.

Paterson, Katherine. **Jacob Have I Loved.** HarperCollins, 1980, 244pp. Grades 6 & Up. A Newbery Award winner.

Realistic fiction. *Ethics; religion; responsibility; rivalry; self-identity.*

Hate. That was the forbidden word.

I hate my sister. I know I shouldn't hate anyone. I'm a Methodist. I belong to a religion that teaches me that to hate someone makes me liable to the judgment of God. To hate is the equivalent of murder.

I hate my twin sister as the biblical Jacob hated Esau. Like Caroline and I, Esau and Jacob were twins. Jacob was the favored twin, just like Caroline.

I'm like the biblical twin Esau. I'm plain and ordinary. Caroline is bright like Jacob. No wonder I hate her.

How can I get rid of these sinful thoughts?

Paulsen, Gary. **Canyons.** Bantam Doubleday Dell Books for Young People, 1990, 184pp. Grades 6 & Up.

Mystery/thrillers. *Abuse; death; Native Americans; time travel.*

How real are our dreams? That question haunts 15-year-old Brennan.

Brennan discovers a human skull in a public camping area. Without telling anyone, he takes it home and puts it by his bed. That night he has the strangest dream about an Apache boy named Coyote Runs. Coyote Runs and his tribe raid Army camps to steal horses. One day Coyote Runs is captured by some cavalry men and is executed. His body is left in a canyon.

This dream disturbs Brennan so he takes the skull to a forensic specialist. The specialist confirms Brennan's dream. The skull belonged to an adolescent Apache male who had been killed by a bullet between the eyes.

Brennan knows the dreams will continue until he takes action. What should he do?

Paulsen, Gary. **Hatchet.** Macmillan, 1989, 152pp. Grades 6 & Up. First in a series: **The River** and **Brian's Winter** follow.

Adventure. *Men's issues; problem parents; sex and sexuality; survival.*

 *This series is a favorite with middle school students. This book's sequel, **The River**, is about Brian's return to the area to make a TV documentary. Due to adverse conditions, he must relive the horror. **Brian's Winter** is what would have happened to Brian if he hadn't been rescued.*

"Chest! My chest is coming apart!"

Brian knew the pilot was having a heart attack. Brian watched helplessly as the plane plunged 7,000 feet. All alone with a dead pilot.

Somehow, Brian knew to pull back on the wheel to increase the plane's altitude. It rose so quickly that Brian's stomach lurched. Brian eventually settled the plane.

The radio, of course! At first Brian contacted someone, but he lost the connection. All he could think to do was to hold the altitude and try the radio every few minutes. As time passed, he knew he would have to eventually glide down, find a body of water to cushion the blow, and land.

As the plane hit the water, he prepared for the worst. If he did survive, the only tool he had was a hatchet.

Peck, Richard. **Bel-Air Bambi and the Mall Rats.** Delacorte, 1993, 183pp. Grades 6-9.

Humor. *Crime; rivalry; show business.*

Bambi Babcock is no bimbo, even if she does come from Bel-Air and is blonde. Neither is her younger sister, Buffie, or her brother, Brick. However, the Babcock kids may be a bit strange from all those years of acting in the unsold TV pilots that their parents direct and produce. Now their dad is out of a job, and they need to get out of town fast.

The Babcocks move from Bel-Air in Los Angeles to Hickory Fork. They are hoping to move away from crime and delinquency. Wrong! A teenage gang called the Mall Rats has taken over the school and the town.

Bambi plans to exterminate the Mall Rats once and for all. Join the hilarious battle of wits between *Bel-Air Bambi and the Mall Rats.*

Perkins, Mitali. **The Sunita Experiment.** Little, Brown, 1993, 179pp. Grades 6 & Up.

Realistic fiction. *Immigrants; India and Pakistan; peer pressure; problem parents; religious prejudice; self-identity.*

Sunita Sen thinks she has a weird family. As she says, "Is there any home in America today where boys are not allowed to come over? Where a girl practically has to beg to spend the night at her best friend's house? Where people eat with their hands and wear sheets in public?"

Sunita's family is originally from India. She feel increasingly embarrassed by their customs. When her grandparents from India visit her family, Sunita decides to avoid her boyfriend, Michael. After all, Michael comes from an American family and would be uncomfortable around Sunita's "weird" family.

Sunita's shame keeps her from friends and a social life. Eventually she must face the one person from whom she is running–herself.

Peyton, K. M. **Snowfall.** (Pbk.) Scholastic, 1994, 360pp. Grades 8 & Up.

Realistic fiction. *Death; Europe; friendship; love; sports (mountain climbing); work.*

When Charlotte was young, she sought adventure and love. A trip to the Alps seemed the perfect escape from a loveless marriage to an elderly rich man. How right she was. She formed solid friendships with Phyllida, Clara, Kitty, and Mar. She found love with Casmir, the tourist guide. She became infatuated with Milo Rawnsley, a rich English gentleman who invited the group to become his household staff.

Milo proposed that the group meet again in the Alps at the age of 75. At the appointed year, changed by time, the friends returned to the Alps. One person was missing. Those returning friends faced a terrible tragedy. A body was discovered that had been missing for more than 50 years!

Pfieffer, Susan Beth. **The Ring of Truth.** Bantam, 1993. Grades 7 & Up.

Realistic fiction. *Ethics; politics; rivalry; sex and sexuality; sexual abuse; women's issues.*

 Give some background on "sexual politics," including the legal meaning of sexual harassment. This book is a good companion to Avi's **Nothing But the Truth** *and the Colliers'* **The Clock**.

Sloane Fredericks is part of a well-known political family from Washington, D.C. At one of her grandmother's political gatherings, Sloane is privately approached by lieutenant governor Mark Heiler. He tries to kiss her, but she rejects his advances.

Sloane indiscreetly tells some friends. Shortly afterwards Sloane's secret appears in a Washington tabloid. Sloane is humiliated by the inference that she had an affair with the lieutenant governor. Sloane knows her best friend, Justine, is the one who was once involved with Mark. That's what Justine says anyway. Is this the truth or another figment of Justine's imagination?

For the whole truth and nothing but, try *The Ring of Truth.*

Philbrick, Rodman. **Freak the Mighty.** Blue Sky/Scholastic, 1993, 169pp. Grades 6 & Up. An ALA Best Books for Young Adults selection.

Realistic fiction. *Death; disability (physical and mental); friendship; movie novels; trust.*

The brain and the brawn.

I never had a brain until Freak came along and let me borrow his for awhile. Freak never really had a body he could use so I let him borrow mine for awhile. I let him do all the talking except when I wanted to say something with my fists. Together we became Freak the Mighty, slaying dragons and fools and walking high above the world. It was easy to put Freak on my shoulders to haul him around, using his brain and my brawn.

Freak the Mighty was pretty cool, if I do say so myself. See if you agree.

Phipson, Joan. **Hit and Run.** Methuen, 1986, 117pp. Grades 6 & Up.

Realistic fiction. *Crime; ethics; problem parents; responsibility; survival.*

Roland didn't mean to hit the baby as he was speeding in the red Ferrari. It was an accident. Still, what else could he do? He had to drive away because if he stopped, his father would find out. His father already thought he was a loser, and his father was always right. He was one of the richest and most powerful men in Australia.

Gordon, an off-duty police officer, saw the hit-and-run accident. Gordon followed Roland in a high-speed chase to arrest him. Then the second accident happened. This time, Gordon and his car were seriously damaged. To survive, Gordon must trust Roland to radio the police for help.

Will Roland leave Gordon to die? Will Roland run away again from a problem?

Plummer, Louise. **The Unlikely Romance of Kate Bjorkman.** Delacorte, 1995, 183pp. Grades 6 & Up.

Romance. *Love; rivalry; women's issues.*

I really hate romance novels. You know, the gross kind with a muscle-bound man falling passionately in love with a maiden named Fleur. Those romances are sappy in the extreme.

This romance really happened. It's lasted six weeks so far, and that's a record for me.

So sit back and relax. I'm Kate Bjorkman, and I'm ready to give romance my best shot. Here's my love story with Richard Bradshow, the guy I've been in love with practically all my 16 years.

Powell, Randy. **Is Kissing a Girl Who Smokes Like Kissing an Ashtray?** Farrar, Strauss & Giroux, 1992, 199pp. Grades 7 & Up. An ALA Best Books for Young Adults selection.

Realistic fiction. *Love; sex and sexuality; substance abuse (cigarettes and marijuana).*

Is kissing a girl who smokes like licking an ashtray?

Hey, I need to know. I'm 18, and I should know. I look four years younger so I don't. I've never had a girlfriend, so I just don't know these things.

I really like this girl, Tommie Isaac, but I just can't seem to talk to her. Follow her around, secretly stalk her, yes. Talk to her, no. I'm not a weirdo either, just embarrassed.

I'm friends with this goofball named Heidi who smokes like a chimney. Heidi thinks I'm nuts for freezing like an icicle when Tommie is around. Heidi is pretty cool–in spite of her nicotine habit. Me, I'm a recovering pinball addict, so I can relate.

Back to the subject: Is kissing a girl who smokes like licking an ashtray? Answer: I don't know. I've never licked one.

Pulman, Philip. **The Ruby in the Smoke.** Alfred Knopf, 1987, 230pp. Grades 6 & Up. First in the *Sally Lockhart Trilogy:* **Shadow of the North** and **The Tiger in the Well** follow.

Mysteries/thrillers. *Crime; revenge; secrets; survival.*

On a cold afternoon in early October 1872, a horse-drawn cab pulled up outside the law offices of Lockhart and Selby. A young girl stepped out the pay the driver.

She was 16 and uncommonly pretty. Her name was Sally Lockhart. Within 15 minutes, she was going to murder a man.

Sally asked the attorney two questions about her father's death by drowning. Who was Mr. Machganes? What did the phrase "the Seven Blessings" mean? The attorney died of fright before answering.

Pursued by villains and cutthroats, Sally resolved to solve the mystery of her father's death. Join her on her excursion to find the ruby in the smoke.

Regan, Dian Curtis. Princess Nevermore. (Pbk.) Scholastic, 1995, 232pp. Grades 6 & Up.

Fantasy. *Love; magic; school; supernatural.*

Do you believe in magic?

Princess Quinnella is surrounded by magic. Her favorite place is the wishing pool. She loves to look up and view the outer world called Earth. The wizard Melikar warns the Princess of the sad people on Earth. These humans throw their pennies into the pool just to have one wish granted.

Nevertheless, Princess Quinn longs to visit this magical place called Earth. One day her wish comes true. She doesn't quite fit into Caprock High School, with her regal mannerisms and her archaic speech. For example, she calls a dance a "ball." She describes her long golden hair as "tresses." She even falls in love with a mere mortal.

Princess Quinn doesn't belong on Earth. How can she return to her kingdom below the wishing pool? Is she destined to be Princess Nevermore?

Rinaldi, Ann. The Last Silk Dress. Holiday, 1988. 368pp. Grades 6 & Up.

Historical fiction. *Civil War; interracial relations; love; problem parents; secrets.*

Susan Dobson Chilmark needs some excitement in her life. Okay, so it's 1860, and the Confederacy has declared war on the Union. That's exciting. However, Susan's strict mother keeps a tight rein on Susan. After all, Richmond, Virginia, is the capitol of the Confederacy, and the city has all kinds of riffraff.

For excitement Susan likes to put on her brother's clothes and sneak out of the house. During one of Susan's secretive adventures, she is kidnapped by a handsome man. He roughly throws her into his carriage and demands to know what she is doing wearing his clothes!

Could this be Susan's long-lost brother, Lucius? Years ago Lucius and her father had such a bitter argument that Lucius left the house, never to return. Local gossip says that her brother now runs a successful brothel and casino.

From this day forward Susan's life will embrace excitement, adventure, and, yes, even romance.

Rinaldi, Ann. A Stitch in Time (The Quilt Trilogy). Scholastic, 1994, 304pp. Grades 7 & Up. Part of a series, including: **Broken Days** and **The Blue Door.**

Historical fiction. *Family; love; problem parents; secrets.*

Secrets, secrets, secrets. In 1779 the Chelmsford family is hiding many secrets. These secrets are destroying the family.

First, the oldest sister, Abigail, plans to elope secretly with a sailor, Nate Videau. Next, Hannah rejects a suitor, who returns from the West with a half-breed daughter he wants Hannah to raise. The youngest sister, Thankful, escapes to the West, only to be captured by Indians. Their father is hiding the most dangerous secret of all: Their deceased mother had a serious relationship with a British soldier.

Like a quilt, once these secrets unravel, the fabric of the family could be destroyed forever.

Rinaldi, Ann. **Time Enough for Drums.** (Pbk.) Troll, 1986, 249pp. With bibliography. Grades 6 & Up.

Historical fiction. *Love; American Revolutionary War; secrets.*

I can't believe that my family is allowing John Reid to tutor me. John Reid is a Tory and a bully!

My family has always supported the American Revolution. My mother writes anonymous letters in support of the Rebels. My father, a merchant, refuses to sell tea after the Boston Tea Party. My brother Dan is a soldier for the Rebel cause. My younger brother, David, wants to enlist when he comes of age.

So why does my family employ this bully to tutor me? No one is more surprised than I when I discover John Reid's secret. Then I have no other choice but to fall in love with him!

Rinaldi, Ann. **Wolf by the Ears.** (Pbk.) Scholastic, 1991, 252pp. Grades 7 & Up. A Senior Readers' Choice Award winner.

Historical fiction. *African Americans; interracial relations; secrets.*

I am not a slave. I don't care what anyone says. I don't believe my friend Thurston, my mother Sally Hemmings, or even my father Thomas Jefferson. I am not a slave. I have a tutor. I am well dressed. I do very little work. How can I be a slave?

Yet that must be what I am. My mother wants me to escape up North to freedom, but I would be running away from everybody and everything I love.

What should I do?

Robert, Willo Davis. **The View from the Cherry Tree.** Macmillan, 1975, 190pp.; (Pbk.) Macmillan, 1987. Grades 6 & Up.

Mysteries/thrillers. *Crime; death; revenge.*

The view from the cherry tree allowed Rob to see many interesting things. However, he never dreamed he would witness a murder! Yet that's exactly what happened. Mrs. Calloway fell out of her window and hanged herself in the cherry tree with her binocular straps. "A bizarre accident" was the general consensus in the neighborhood.

Only Rob knew that Mrs. Calloway was pushed out of the window during a heated argument. From his view in the cherry tree, Rob saw hands striking and throttling the old woman.

Rob tried to solve the mystery by a systematic investigation. However, the murderer learned about Rob's investigation and was out to destroy Rob first!

Ross, Ramon Royal. **Harper and Moon.** Atheneum, 1993, 181pp. Grades 7-9.

Mysteries/thrillers. *Death; disability (mental); secrets.*

Someone has killed Harper's friend Olinger. Whoever it was is stalking Harper, too. Harper can run or he can stall. Either way he is caught.

Wait a minute. That stalker has a familiar walk. Thank goodness, it's Moon! Even though Moon can be mentally slow at times, he might help Harper bury Olinger's body.

Wait a minute. How long has Moon been watching him? Why hadn't Moon told Harper he was there? Just what is going on?

Roybal, Laura. **Billy.** Houghton Mifflin, 1994, 231pp. Grades 6 & Up.

Realistic fiction. *Men's issues; problem parents; secrets; self-identity; trust.*

 Note: *There are several excellent books on changed identities, such as* **My Name is Eddie Leonard***, by Harry Mazer, and* **The Face on the Milk Carton***, by Caroline Cooney. These books could be booktalked as books about kidnapping.*

What would it be like to lose your identity at 10 and then to lose it again at 16?

When Billy was 10, he was kidnapped from a baseball game. The kidnapper turned out to be his father, whom Billy had never met. Billy's father convinced him that his stepfather never wanted him and would never try to find him.

Six years pass. Billy has begun living a fast-paced life in a small New Mexican town. When Billy is arrested in a bar brawl, he is told that his fingerprints have been computer-matched to those of a missing child. Billy Melendez is now to become William Campbell again. He will go to Iowa to live with his mother and stepfather.

If Billy Melendez does change his name to William Campbell, will he stop being Billy? Just who is the real Billy anyway?

Sharpe, Susan. **Real Friends.** Bradbury, 1994, 167pp. Grades 6 & Up.

Realistic fiction. *Friendship; peer pressure; rivalry.*

Who are your real friends? That's what Cassie Mason wants to know.

Cassie doesn't have many friends because she is part of a military family that moves from place to place. Cassie has lived in Panama, Germany, and Egypt. Now she's back in the United States, going to an American school.

After two months, Cassie has only one person she can claim as a friend. Just like Cassie, Susan Carpenter is a goody-goody worry-wart. Then Helen comes into Cassie's life. Unlike Susan, Helen would rather party than do homework. Little by little, Helen takes over Cassie's life until Cassie is unable to make new friends.

Is Helen a real friend?

Sherman, Josepha. **Windleaf.** Walkerland, 1993, 121pp. Grades 6 & Up.

Fantasy. *Love; magic; occult; supernatural.*

I am Glinfinial. In English my name means Windleaf. I am half-human, half-faerie.

My father, Tiernathal, hates humans, perhaps because in his perceived weakness he fell in love with my human mother. He curses the day his tribe of faeries entered the Gate between the Realms into Human Land. Tricked by that treacherous mortal Time, they have forgotten the way back to Faerie. They are forever exiles in Human Land.

Father warned me about the inferiority of Humans. I believed him until I met the young count Thierry. Ah, such a wonder is he. He takes delight of me, also. We vow to stay together until eternity. My father's spells pull me back to the twilight realm, yet I am confident that my lover will follow me to battle the unknown.

Therefore, dear reader, join me on our journey of adventure and romance to discover if love truly conquers all.

Skurzynski, Gloria. **Virtual War.** Simon & Schuster for Young People, 1997, 152pp. Grades 6 & Up. An ALA Best Books for Young Readers selection.

Science fiction. *Computers; disability (physical); end-of-the-world; survival; war.*

"I pledge to wage the War with courage, dedication, and honor."

Corgan has said this pledge many times. After all, the War is only 18 days away. He is prepared for the virtual war.

Then he meets a beautiful girl, named Sharla, who is to be his partner in the War. She assures Corgan she is real, but could anyone that beautiful be real?

Sharla is definitely real. A real rebel. Each night she sneaks out of her Box to explore the city. The Supreme Council forces her into Reprimand, but Sharla is the world's best code breaker so the Supreme Council must employ her skills.

Next, Brig joins the group. He's a 10-year-old Mutant, who happens to be a genius. He plans the strategy of the virtual war.

Now, the three have joined forces to fight two battles. One battle is a computer-controlled virtual war. The other battle is contained within themselves. Can they learn to think independently without automatically obeying the Supreme Council?

Will they win both wars?

Sleator, William. **The Duplicate.** Dutton, 1988, 160pp.; (Pbk.) Bantam, 1990. Grades 6 & Up.

Horror. *Revenge; rivalry; supernatural; survival.*

Have you ever wished for a duplicate or a clone? Have you ever wanted to have someone who looks and acts just like you? That way you could be in two places at the same time.

David wishes he had a duplicate. By duplicating himself, he could visit Grandma and keep his date with Angela.

One lucky day he discovers a "Spee-Dee-Dupe" on the beach. He was able to duplicate himself. What luck!

Really, though, how lucky is it to possess a duplicate? The situation begins turning into a nightmare with deadly consequences. This human clone wants to assume David's life—permanently!

Sleator, William. **Oddballs.** Dutton, 1993, 134pp. Grades 6 & Up.

Humor. *Ethics; family; friendship; self-identity.*

 This booktalk is successful with teenagers. Maybe they appreciate a family of nonconformists. Incidentally, the "unexpected result" of The Pitiful Encounter is that the handsome boys sincerely ask the plain Avis to a party that night. They appear to be totally uninterested in the pretty girls.

Meet the oddballs–the Sleator family.

Meet Dad, a physiologist who invites his family to inspect dead bodies in the university lab. Meet Mom, a pediatrician who refuses to give her fourth child a name until he is two years old. Finally Mom names him Tycho Barney George Clement Newby Sleator!

The Sleators and their friends delight in being different. One game their friends play is called "The Pitiful Encounter." The friends would board a city bus. Two of the friends were beautiful girls. They would pretend to humiliate one of their uglier friends–usually Avis, who was in on the gag. The friends would enjoy observing the public's reaction.

"You're ugly, you can't be our friend."

"I want to be your friend," Avis would whine.

"No way, you're just too ugly."

The Pitiful Encounter would usually provoke a strong reaction from the riders on the bus. Sometimes they would become angry at the "cruelty" of the girls. Once a compassionate traveler gave Avis some money!

However, one day Avis is approached by three handsome college boys, and this Pitiful Encounter has some unexpected results . . .

Sleator, William. **Singularity.** E. P. Dutton, 1985. Grades 6 & Up. An ALA Best Books for Young Adults selection.

Science fiction. *Rivalry; supernatural; time travel.*

What is a singularity? Good question. A singularity is a star that has collapsed, creating a gravitational pull so strong not even light can escape from it. A singularity is also known as a *black hole.*

Got that? Okay, what if this singularity has two sides? One side would speed up time and the other side would slow down time. What if one side of a singularity is somewhere on earth?

Sound fantastic? The twins Harry and Barry didn't believe this, either. Then they found the end of a singularity. This magical tunnel of time was located inside a house their family inherited.

What is inside this singularity? Is there another universe on the other side? When the twins enter the singularity, they certainly didn't plan to meet a mysterious deadly force.

Could this evil force destroy the earth? How dangerous is this singularity?

Staples, Suzanne Fisher. **Shabanu: Daughter of the Wind.** Alfred A. Knopf, 1989, 240pp. Grades 7 & Up. A Newbery Honor book; an ALA Best Book for Young Adults selection.

Realistic fiction. *India and Pakistan; pregnancy; religious prejudice; rites of passage; women's issues.*

 This book is difficult to categorize because it defies genres and topics. The author simply and directly tells the story of two teenage Muslim girls who are forced into arranged marriages. The author's sequel, **Haveli**, *is also excellent, but for more mature readers. That booktalk is on page 127.*

I am Shabanu, daughter of the wind. Mama says I have the name of a princess, but my family is nomadic. We roam the Pakistan desert with our camels and other animals.

My older sister, Phulan, is 13 and engaged to be married. Next year I will be married to Murad. Mama says both marriages are a good match because both of the men own land.

Sometimes Phulan and I are afraid of the future. We have always known our fate, but sometimes we long for the right to choose our destiny.

What will become of us?

Stolz, Mary. **Cezanne Pinto: A Memoir.** Alfred A. Knopf, 1994, 279pp. Grades 6 & Up.

Historical fiction. *African Americans; aging; animals (horses); Civil War; interracial relations; pioneer life; racism.*

I'm Cezanne Pinto, a former slave.

In 1860, when I ran away from the plantation in Virginia, I decided to be 12 years old. Could have been anywhere from 10 to 14. As the great Frederick Douglass said, you might as well ask a horse how old he is as a slave. Now I'm pushing the 90 mark. Or am I? Don't matter now.

Anyhow, Cezanne Pinto ain't my slave name. I took it on when I run away. Another slave, named Tamar, run away with me on the Underground Railroad. She teached me to speak proper English and to read and write. Went to Canada, then joined up with the Union Army. Then I became a cowboy in Texas.

I've put it all down. There now, I believe I'll lie down for a spell.

Tamar, Erika. **The Truth about Kim O'Hara.** Atheneum, 1992, 186pp. Grades 6 & Up. Second in a series: **It Happened at Ceceila's** precedes.

Realistic fiction. *Abuse; Asian Americans; secrets; Vietnam War.*

The truth about Kim O'Hara is that she's carrying a deep, dark secret. At first Andy Szabo is only aware of her Asian-American beauty. Andy has had a crush on her since ninth grade. Then he gets to know her. He observes Kim's relentless drive to be perfect, her rigid self-control, and her inability to relax. Her reactions don't make sense to him at all. Kim seems to have such loving and easygoing parents. When he discovers her secret, when he learns the truth about Kim O'Hara, then he understands.

Van der Rol, Ruud & Dian Verhoeven, for the Anne Frank House. **Anne Frank: Beyond the Diary, A Photographic Remembrance.** Introduction by Anna Quindlen. Viking, 1993, 113pp. Grades 6 & Up.

Biography. *Europe (Holland); Holocaust; Jews; religious prejudices; survival; World War II.*

 Note: This book is an excellent introduction to Anne Frank and can be used for all ages. *The Diary of Anne Frank* could be read after this introduction to her life.

Dear Kitty,

Everyone begins a diary that says "Dear Diary." I am definitely not everyone. I'm not like my perfect sister or my irritating mother. I'm not even like my father whom I adore. No, I am just me, Anne Frank. I'm a Jew hiding in Amsterdam with my family during World War II.

Look at these pictures. Learn about my life. Maybe one day you can read my diary or visit my hiding place in Amsterdam.

As different as I like to be, in many ways am I similar to you?

Anne Frank

Tunis, John. **The Kid from Tomkinsville.** Harcourt, Brace, Jovanovich, 1940. Grades 6 & Up.

Sports. *Aging; disability (physical); sports (baseball).*

 Note: All of John Tunis's books are excellent. Some of them are out of print. If you see them in a used bookstore or can obtain them elsewhere, you won't regret it.

"Ya know how you make it in the Big Leagues, kid?" said Dodger's catcher Dave Leonard. "I've been playing baseball in the Big League for 20 years. I've seen them come and go. It doesn't take great talent or skill, like you might think. It takes courage. Courage to make mistakes and to keep trying even when you feel like giving up."

Nineteen-year-old Roy Tucker always remembered Dave Leonard's words. Roy pitched a great first game, but then he suffered an injury that threatened to end his career before it had a chance to begin. Now he needs all the courage that Dave was talking about, the courage to continue on with his career and life.

Vande Velde, Vivian. **Companions of the Night.** Harcourt Brace, 1995, 212pp. Grades 7 & Up. An ALA Best Books for Young Adults selection.

Horror. *Occult; secrets; supernatural; trust.*

Kerry and Ethan become companions of the night. Not by choice, you understand. They are forced to stay together. Ethan is a vampire tortured by sunlight. Kerry is looking for her missing family. Together they join forces as companions of the night.

Of course, Kerry's fear is that she will become one of Ethan's victims. She tries not to fall asleep on their long journey through deadly swamps and dark tunnels. She tries to learn Ethan's background as a vampire so she can stay alive. The only problem is that Ethan can't be trusted, as he tells lie after lie about himself.

Will Kerry be able to survive with her companion of the night?

Vande Velde, Vivian. **Dragon's Bait.** Harcourt Brace, 1992, 131pp. Grades 6 & Up. An ALA Best Books for Young Adults selection.

Fantasy. *Magic; Middle Ages; revenge; supernatural; trust.*

 *This book has the flavor of a twisted fairy tale.*

The day Alys was accused of being a witch started out like any other. By the end of the day, Alys was left as dragon bait by the village people.

Then the dragon arrived. Selendrile was no ordinary dragon. He was golden and could change into human form. His purple eyes gleamed with amusement when Alys bitterly wished for revenge on the village people. Revenge was Selendrile's favorite sport.

Together Selendrile and Alys planned to destroy the village and the people within it.

Alys knew the dragon was not be trusted. When Selendrile finally gets his delight in revenge, will Alys be dragon bait?

Vogel, Ilse-Margret. **Bad Times, Good Friends.** Harcourt, Brace, Jovanovich, 1992, 239pp. Grades 6 & Up.

Biography. *Europe (Germany); homosexuality; Jews; politics; religious prejudice; World War II.*

Bad times were in Berlin in Nazi Germany. Luckily, I had many good friends that hated Nazis as much as I did. We were not super heroes. We were only ordinary people who did small things to make life easier for the persecuted.

I'm Ilse-Margret Vogel. It has taken me 50 years to write this true story because it is still painful to think of my friends who struggled to overthrow Nazi Germany. Perhaps it is necessary to tell you of my painful experiences so that you understand that not all Germans during World War II were Nazis.

Let me share the stories of six of my good friends who tried to help others during the bad times.

Wallace, Bill. **Buffalo Gal.** (Pbk.) Minstrel/Pocket, 1992, 185pp. Grades 6 & Up. An ALA Best Books for Young Adults selection.

Historical fiction. *Ecology; love; Native Americans; pioneer life; women's issues.*

It was my mother's idea to go to Texas to save the buffalo. In my opinion, Texas is nothing but dust, wide-open spaces, and outlaws. Maybe in 50 years, in 1954 or so, civilized people might live in Texas.

However, in 1904 we're facing alligators, rattlesnakes, and stampeding buffalo. What's even worse we're with David Talltree, a half-Comanche cowboy who believes females should leave "men's work" to men.

I expected adventure. I hadn't planned on danger or romance!

Wersba, Barbara. **You'll Never Guess the End.** HarperCollins Children's Books, 1992, 132pp. Grades 6-9.

Mysteries/thrillers. *Crime; rivalry.*

Joel is having a small, silent nervous breakdown. His parents don't notice because they are absorbed in following their older son's thriving career. Joel's older brother, JJ, has just written a best-selling novel, and the family is caught up in his success.

While fame and acclaim overwhelm JJ, his ex-girlfriend, Marilyn, is kidnapped. Only Joel devises a plan to get her back alive.

You'll never guess the end!

Williams, Michael. **Crocodile Burning.** Lodestar, 1992, 198pp. Grades 6 & Up. An ALA Best Books for Young Adults selection.

Realistic fiction. *Apartheid; racism; show business; South Africa.*

Seraki Mandindi lives in the black township of Soweto in Johannesburg, South Africa. His neighborhood is as threatening as a crocodile with its huge jaws ready to take down an innocent victim. The neighborhood consists of gangs and criminals ready to strike their next victim.

When Seraki becomes part of a successful theatrical group that goes on tour to New York, he confronts another crocodile. This crocodile represents the victimization of the actors as they advance from Soweto to Broadway. Is their producer taking financial advantage of them through intimidation and threats?

It's a new day in South Africa. It's also a new day for inexperienced actors to take control of their lives. It's a day for crocodile burning!

Rita Williams-Garcia. **Fast Talk on a Slow Track.** Bantam, 1992, 182pp. Grades 7 & Up. An ALA Best Books for Young Adults selection.

Realistic fiction. *African Americans; responsibility; rites of passage; school.*

Denzel Watson is one smooth-talking dude. He's so smooth he could sell apples to a toothless guy. You should hear him sell candy bars, especially the cool way he uses his phony African accent to get attention. That's when he uses his real name, Dinizulu, instead of the name Denzel, a name he adopted after he saw actor Denzel Washington.

Denzel is slick in school, too. He is even selected as valedictorian of his senior class. Denzel has studying down to a science. He glances at the pages of a book without reading. In no time he learns the main characters, plot, and theme. Hey, school is no sweat for fast-talking Denzel.

Things change when Denzel attends the summer program for minority students at Princeton, one of the top Ivy League schools. This fast-talking dude cannot smooth talk his way through any of his classes.

How will Denzel cope? Will he continue his fast talk on a slow track?

Wittlinger, Ellen. **Lombardo's Law.** Houghton Mifflin, 1993, 137pp. Grades 6-9.

Romance. *Love; peer pressure.*

 This book is a light, harmless romance similar to Claudia Mill's **Dinah In Love**.

I've got a problem.

The Lombardos have moved across the street. I tried to be friends with Heather, but she's too much of an airhead. It's her younger brother, Mike, I've come to know and like.

That's my problem. How can I possibly like a kid who's two years younger and a couple of inches shorter? I mean, we both have the same sense of humor and like the same movies, but get real! He's just a kid!

What's a girl to do about this embarrassing situation?

Wrede, Patricia C. **Dealing with Dragons: The Enchanted Forest Chronicles, Book One.** Scholastic, 1990. Grades 6 & Up. First in a series: **Searching for Dragons; Calling on Dragons;** and **Talking to Dragons** follow.

Fantasy. *Magic; occult; responsibility; supernatural; women's issues.*

 Note: This fantasy twists a few fairy tales, as well.

Take one very bored princess who runs away from a prearranged marriage to a very dull prince. Add one dangerous dragon who allows the princess to cook and perform other household tasks. Together they provide humor and excitement in an enchanted forest filled with witches, wizards, and wicked giants.

Will Cimorene, princess of the dragon Kuzul, be able to stop the wizards from collecting the deadly plant dragonsbane? Will the enchanted stone prince find a princess to break the spell and live happily ever after?

Try this topsy-turvy tale about dealing with dragons.

Malcolm X. **Malcolm X Talks to Young People: Speeches in the U.S., Great Britain and Africa.** Pathfinder, 1991, 110pp. Grades 7 & Up.

Nonfiction. *African Americans; ethics; politics; racism; responsibility.*

I am Malcolm X. I was born Malcolm Little in 1926, but I deleted my last name because "Little" is a slave name. I have no idea of my real African name. So I use "X" as the unknown.

People say I am controversial. Yes, I do believe in a revolution of the mind. It's time we put our prejudices aside and look at our political leaders clearly. Are our leaders protecting our civil and human rights? I feel people in power have misused their power. Now there has to be a change. The only way the change will occur is with extreme methods: a revolution of the mind.

I invite anyone to join this revolution of the mind with me. I don't care what color you are as long as you want to change the miserable conditions that exist on this earth.

I'm asking you to open your mind and let me enter.

Yolen, Jane. **The Devil's Arithmetic.** Viking, 1988, 170pp. Grades 6 & Up. An ALA Best Books for Young Adults selection.

Historical fiction. *Europe (Poland); Holocaust; Jews; religious prejudice; survival; time travel; World War II.*

Hannah is tired of going to her family's Passover dinner. She's tired of hearing her relatives' stories about the Holocaust. How she wishes her parents wouldn't insist that she go.

During the Passover Seder, Hannah is transported back in time to 1942, to a Polish village where everyone calls her Chaya.

Suddenly Nazi soldiers arrive. Unfortunately, Hannah/Chaya knows what lies ahead.

Booktalks for High School And Adults (Grades 9 & Up)

These books are an odd assortment, a mixture of the old and the new, the classic and the controversial. These booktalks are for the mature reader. This includes older students, teachers, administrators, and parents.

Some of the selections of books may surprise you. They include literary classics by Ernest Hemingway, Ray Bradbury, Aldous Huxley, and Carson McCullers. These books have endured and are still in print. However, when recommending books to teenagers, don't refer to the book as a "classic." Many teenagers have a negative response to that word.

Also included are standards of young adult and children's literature. These books by L. M. Montgomery, Mark Twain, and Harper Lee are still being read today. They can be used "for all ages" in that they can be read aloud to younger readers. When choosing a read-aloud, select the book based upon the maturity of the reader. The more mature the reader, the more the reader will appreciate the complexity of the book. Reading aloud also

allows discussion about any complex issues that are in the book.

Use discretion when recommending controversial books to a young reader. The less mature reader may find such books offensive or upsetting. Many of these books share complex themes and subjects. Some deal with mature subjects, such as sexual abuse and homosexuality. At times, profanity may be explicit. My notes at the end of the booktalk will explore these issues.

Recommend these books to teachers and other adults. A school library media center should have a fiction collection for teachers, even in elementary schools. The best-sellers and classics should be included. Teachers should have easy access to these books, even if the books are informally exchanged rather than bought. Occasionally you might want to do short booktalks to large groups of faculty or parents.

It doesn't matter how you get these books into a reader's hands. Just make certain they are exposed to the best. These books are some favorites for the pure pleasure of reading.

Book
Talks!

Angelou, Maya. **The Heart of a Woman.** Random House, 1981, 272pp. Grades 9 & Up. Part of a series, including: **I Know Why the Caged Bird Sings; Gather Together in My Name; Singin' and Swingin' and Gettin' Merry Like Christmas** precede; **All God's Children Need Traveling Shoes** follows. Oprah Winfrey book selection.

Biography. *Africa; African Americans; apartheid; show business; single parents; work; women's issues.*

Maya Angelou wears many hats. She's a political activist, singer, dancer, poet, and writer. Her book *I Know Why the Caged Bird Sings* is now a classic coming-of-age story about her life in Mississippi.

The Heart of a Woman is the fourth book in her autobiographical series. This is an account of her encounters with some fascinating people. She knew Dr. Martin Luther King, Malcolm X, singer Billie Holiday, and writers James Baldwin and Rosa Guy. She also writes of her traveling life from New York City to Cairo, Egypt, to Accra, Ghana. Her marriage to a South African activist takes Maya through many different cultures and customs.

Book a seat aboard Maya Angelou's journey of life.

Anonymous. **Go Ask Alice.** Avon Flare, 1971, 189pp. Grades 9 & Up.

Realistic fiction. *Eating disorders; sex and sexuality; sexual abuse; substance abuse (alcohol and drugs).*

Note: This book is both controversial and a classic, as it is still read more than 20 years after being published. There is some dispute as to whether it is an autobiography. It contains profanity, and many sexual issues are directly confronted. For the mature reader, however, this book is unforgettable.

Alice is a drug addict who expresses herself honestly in her diary:

January 24

Anyone who says pot and acid are not addicting is crazy! After you've had it, there isn't even life without drugs. Without drugs, life stinks. I'm glad I'm on drugs. Glad! Glad! Glad!

Yet I've never felt more alone in my life. Sometimes I think I'm losing my mind. Please God, help me.

Arrick, Fran. **What You Don't Know Can Kill You.** Bantam Books for Young Readers, 1992, 154pp. Grades 9 & Up. An ALA Best Books for Young Adults selection.

Realistic fiction. *AIDS; responsibility; sex and sexuality; suicide.*

Everything is going along fine. Then suddenly, a phone call. A doorbell. Something. And your world goes out of whack all of a sudden. Just like that.

When the phone rings, the Geddes family have no idea that their lives would completely change. A family they know has been involved in a car accident. The doctor needs blood. All the Geddes family become blood donors. The family is shocked when 17-year-old Ellen tests HIV positive. Ellen is a good girl. Bad things aren't supposed to happen to good people.

Debra has always envied her older sister Ellen. Now Debra must face losing her sister. The family faces the hostility of the community, especially when Ellen's boyfriend, Jack Ritterhouse, makes a tragic decision.

When it comes to AIDS, what you don't know can kill you.

Bauer, Marion Dane, editor. **Am I Blue? Coming out of the Silence.** HarperTrophy, 1994, 273pp. Grades 9 & Up. An ALA Best Books for Young Adults selection.

Short stories. *AIDS; homosexuality; sex and sexuality.*

Melvin is one of a kind–a "fairy" godfather. He's a guardian angel who used to be gay when he was alive. Now his mission is to show Vince what would happen if every gay person turned blue for a day. That day is an educational experience for Vince–just as it will be for you.

Am I Blue? is just one of many short stories about being gay. Authors such as M. E. Kerr, Francesca Lia Block (of *Weetzie Bat* fame), and Lois Lowry share their stories with us. Some are from the outside, some from the inside.

You'll enjoy these stories, whether or not you're "blue."

Bess, Clayton. **The Mayday Rampage.** Lookout Press, 1993, 198pp. Grades 9 & Up. An ALA Best Books for Young Adults selection.

Realistic fiction. *AIDS; homosexuality; love; men's issues; politics; responsibility; sex and sexuality.*

 Note. This is an excellent groundbreaking book that has a surprise ending, revealing that Molly eventually contracts AIDS. Information about AIDS is contained throughout. This book could even save lives.

People, listen up! We have a beef with authority and we're facing school suspension.

What's up, you ask? We, Jess Judd and Molly Pierce, are journalists for the school newspaper, *The Rampage*. We wrote a series of very frank articles about AIDS. Well, if you're gonna discuss AIDS, you gotta be frank, don't you? Like, people's lives depend on our honesty.

The principal liked our first article. We wrote of six-year-old David Deering, who became infected with AIDS. However, when we started interviewing prostitutes and gays, we got plenty of flak. Plus, the parents weren't too crazy about our advice column, which answered all the questions we thought teenagers should know.

Things got worse on May Day when we anonymously interviewed a teacher who happens to be gay. That's when it really hit the fan!

Blake, Michael. **Dances with Wolves.** Fawcett Gold, 1988, 313pp. Grades 8 & Up.

Historical fiction. *Civil War; love; movie novels; Native Americans; pioneer life; survival.*

Have you seen the movie? Have you read this book?

Dances with Wolves was a huge success for actor and director Kevin Costner. Costner knew the story's author, Michael Blake. Costner promised Blake that he would produce and direct Blake's novel into a movie. Costner kept his promise, and the film won numerous awards.

For those of you who haven't seen the movie or read the book, you will enter the American West during the late 1860s. A drunken major orders Lieutenant John Dunbar to an abandoned army post, where he finds himself alone with only a wolf and horse. Eventually John Dunbar befriends a group of Comanches. When he changes his name to *Dances to Wolves*, he changes his life forever.

Blume, Judy. **Forever.** Pocket Books, 1976, 220pp. Grades 9 & Up. An ALA Best Books for Young Adults selection.

Romance. *Love, responsibility; rites of passage; sex and sexuality.*

 This book by Judy Blume was a breakthrough in young adult literature. The author openly discusses sex and birth control in a young adult novel.

Michael and I are in love. Forever. He even gave me a silver disk necklace that reads "Katherine" on one side and, on the other side, "Michael . . . forever."

Sometimes love can be a pain. My parents want me to be a tennis instructor at a stupid camp in New Hampshire. Now I'll be away from Michael almost all summer. Then we'll be apart during college because we're going to different schools. Will we be separated forever?

One thing does confuse me. I can't understand how can I be attracted to someone else I just met at camp. I thought my love for Michael was forever!

Bogle, Donald. **Dorothy Dandridge: A Biography.** (Pbk.) Boulevard Books, 1998, 612pp. Grades 9 & Up.

Biography. *African Americans; problem parents; racism; show business; women's issues.*

During the 1950s there were two African-American movie stars: Sidney Poitier and Dorothy Dandridge. Dandridge was beautiful, talented, and tragically doomed. Just like Marilyn Monroe, Dorothy Dandridge had it all and lost it all.

Dorothy had more obstacles to overcome than Monroe because segregation was part of American life. Dandridge broke through racial barriers, but the pressure eventually broke her.

Read why Whitney Houston, Halle Berry, and Diana Ross have expressed interest in portraying her life on screen. Read this book before it becomes a movie.

Bradbury, Ray. **The Martian Chronicles.** Doubleday, 1950, 181pp. Grades 8 & Up.

Science fiction. *End-of-the-world; survival; time travel.*

 Sometimes I tell one of the stories because they are chilling, not unlike the television series **The Twilight Zone** *or* **The X Files.** *Don't miss this one even if you think you don't like science fiction.*

"My husband, I had the strangest dream last night. I dreamed men arrived from a place called Earth in something they called a spaceship."

"Really, Ylla, you know the third planet is incapable of supporting life. Scientists say there is too much oxygen."

Mr. and Mrs. K. lived an average Martian life. True, their life could be dull at times, but they were satisfied. Ylla's dream changed all that. Her dream was a prophetic forecast of the future. Strange creatures called Men arrived on Mars!

How could this be? There is no life on the Third Planet, that place the astronauts call Earth. Obviously, these creatures called Earthlings are insane. And on Mars, just like us on Earth, all mentally unbalanced persons must be placed in an insane asylum. But on Mars, if these so-called Earthlings continue their delusions, they must be destroyed!

This story is just one of the bizarre tales from this science fiction classic. Each expedition is weirder than the next. Climb aboard this spaceship to another dimension, not of sight or sound, but of the imagination. Climb aboard *The Martian Chronicles.*

Bragg, Rick. **All Over but the Shouting.** Pantheon Books, 1997, 329pp.; (Pbk.) Vintage, 1998, 326pp. Grades 9 & Up.

Biography. *Class conflict; men's issues; rites of passage; substance abuse (alcohol).*

This story isn't important to anyone but me and a few people who lived it, people with my last name. I'm writing it down because, as one Southern lady told me, "People forgets if it ain't wrote down."

I am, by my very presence, a walking lab, a field trip through the Southern country. Yep, when you're looking at me, you're looking at country. Through and through.

I'm a Pulitzer Prize-winning reporter for the *New York Times*. It was always easier writing about strangers. I didn't think my life as a poor, white Southerner growing up in the Sixties was interesting. I was wrong.

For one thing, I was a murder suspect for an afternoon. A double murder occurred by a man who was obviously insane. The police rounded up everyone who was poor, black, retarded, or had a criminal record. I was poor.

In the South that was the price we all paid for being different.

Braithwaite, E. R. **To Sir with Love.** Heinman Educational Books, 1981. Grades 8 & Up.

Biography. *Great Britain; interracial relations; love; peer pressure; racism; rites of passage; school; sex and sexuality; work.*

"Do you jive?"

Those spoken words are my introduction to life within an East London school. The students are coarse, insolent, and brash.

I don't wish to become a teacher in a London slum. I have no teaching experience or aptitude. Unfortunately, I have no choice. I must work, and the British do not hire black men willingly. This teaching assignment is all I could find after 18 months of unemployment.

After several months of cheekiness from the students, I am no closer to winning respect their respect. One day I walk into the classroom and smell a horrible stench from the grate of the fireplace. Several students are gathered around joking and laughing. I took a closer look at the object that is burning. It is a feminine hygiene product. I am so sickened and disgusted by the students' actions that I lose my temper.

"There are certain things which decent women keep private at all times. Only a filthy slut would do this, and those of you who encouraged her are just as bad. I'm leaving the classroom, during which time that disgusting object will be removed."

As I flee from the classroom, I am discouraged. How can I reach these students?

Slowly an idea occurs to me. Yes, it might work. At least I should try.

Burnett, Frances Hodgson. **The Secret Garden.** With an afterward by Faith McNully. Penguin, 1986, 286pp. First published in 1911. For all ages.

Historical fiction. *Great Britain; illness (physical); movie novels; rites of passage; secrets.*

Mary Lennox had a nickname she detested: "Mary Mary, Quite Contrary." She was, too. Contrary, stubborn, willful, and quite unpleasant.

By being so disagreeable, Mary had no love in her life. Her parents ignored her while they were alive; when they died, Mary didn't miss them. Mary was sent to England to live with her uncle, Archibald Craven, a crusty millionaire. The housekeeper, Mrs. Medlock, also didn't have time to give love to Mary.

Being lonely and alone, Mary discovered the secret garden. Before Mrs. Craven died, her favorite place was the garden. The garden had been locked for years, with vines and weeds hiding the entrance. Mary longed to see the inside of this enchanted garden. If only she could find the key!

Mary also wanted to explore the house of 100 rooms. Were there really 100 rooms, as people said? What was that strange noise that sounded like someone crying?

For the first time, Mary Lennox found her life interesting and even exciting.

Cather, Willa. **My Antonia.** Foreword by Doris Grumbach. Houghton Mifflin, 1988, 322pp. First published in 1918. Grades 8 & Up.

Historical fiction. *Class conflict; immigrants; pioneer life.*

Life was tough in the state of Nebraska in the late 1800s. Many residents were immigrants who came from Norway, Ireland, Sweden, or Russia. These immigrants couldn't speak English or plow a field. So everyone pitched in and helped each other. That's how the narrator, Jim Burden, met his Norwegian neighbor, Antonia Shimerda. Their friendship endured for more than 40 years.

Antonia and Jim loved to gossip about their neighbors. They were fascinated by their two Russian neighbors, Pavel and Peter, who were always together yet always alone. Eventually they heard the gossip about this strange pair.

In Russia Peter and Paval were asked to attend a wedding in the next village. On that cold winter night the wedding party departed by sleigh. Wolves were numerous that winter. Somehow, hundreds of wolves followed the wedding party, and many a driver lost control of his sleigh. Loud shrieks from the people and horses filled the air, as the wolves devoured them.

Pavel and Peter drove the head sleigh, with the groom and bride in the back. As the wolves surrounded the sleigh, Pavel pushed both the groom and bride overboard. The two men made a clean getaway back to their village. When the village people discovered what happened, they banished Pavel and Peter. Shortly afterwards the pair immigrated to America.

For more gossip about their neighbors, read *My Antonia.*

Cisneros, Sandra. **The House on Mango Street.** Vintage Books, 1989, 110pp. Grades 8 & Up.

Short stories. *Class conflict; Hispanic Americans; problem parents; religious prejudice; self-identity.*

Many librarians and teachers recommend this brief, well-written, multicultural book.

We didn't always live on Mango Street. We've moved lots of places until we finally came to own our house. It's no palace. It's tiny, with only one washroom. Everyone has to share a bedroom–Mama and Papa, Carlos and Kiki, me and Nancy.

I'm Esperanza. In English my name means "hope." In Spanish, it means too many letters. It's a sad name to me. A muddy name.

Maybe if I change my name to Lisandra or Zeze the X, I will change my life of poverty, shame, and loneliness.

Clark, Mary Higgins. **Loves Music, Loves to Dance.** (Pbk.) Pocket Books, 1991, 304pp. Grades 9 & Up.

Horror. *Crime; death; illness (mental); revenge.*

"Loves music, loves to dance."
This notice was listed in the personal ad section of the newspaper. It led seven girls to their gruesome deaths, each with a dancing slipper on her right foot.

He wanted to stop killing. The ground was still frozen, and it was dangerous to keep their bodies in the freezer. But Charlie would not let him stop. He said the other two girls who answered the ad must be found. Their pictures revealed dancers' bodies, slender and yet athletic.

He couldn't help fantasizing how much more attractive these two girls would be in just one dancing slipper.

Collier, John Lincoln & Christopher. **With Every Drop of Blood: A Novel of the Civil War.** Delacorte, 1992, 235pp. Grades 9 & Up. An ALA Best Books for Young Adults selection.

Historical fiction. *African Americans; Civil War; interracial relations; men's issues; racism.*

This book is controversial because the authors use the word "nigger," claiming that it was the word used during the time. Nevertheless, this is a well-written and authentic account.

This here Civil War shore muddles the mind. How come some people are fighting those Yanks for one reason and some for another? To be straight, I weren't shore all us Rebels are as hot for States' rights and the Constitution as Pa were. I never heerd much talk of it from the soldiers.

Me, I wanted to fight them no-good Yanks because they killed my Pa. I promised Pa 'fore he died that I would not run off and enlist. I swore I wouldn't leave my sisters and Ma unprotected at home. But, Pa, what about my duty to my state, Virginny?

Pa, what if I go teamstering with my mules and wagon? That ain't the same, is it, Pa?

Dadblame it, Pa, if I ain't got myself captured by a black soldier!

Conroy, Pat. **Beach Music.** (Pbk.)
Bantam Books, 1996, 780pp.
Grades 9 & Up.

Realistic fiction. *Men's issues; secrets; sex and sexuality; substance abuse; suicide.*

In 1979 my wife leapt to her death from the Silas Pearlman Bridge in Charleston, South Carolina. A year later I packed up my toddler daughter Leah and moved us to Italy to begin life anew.

For me, the South was carry-on baggage I could not shed, no matter how many borders I crossed. Without realizing it, I made the mistake of turning South Carolina into a secret paradise to my daughter. Leah longed to return to her birthplace and my place of agony. In 1985 I gave up the ghost and returned to Charleston, to my past, to my agony.

My memories are covered with hidden land mines, but I must risk this journey for my daughter and for my peace of mind. God help both of us.

Conroy, Pat. **The Prince of Tides.**
(Pbk.) Houghton Mifflin, 1986, 664pp.
Grades 9 & Up.

Realistic fiction. *Abuse; men's issues; movie novels; sexual abuse; substance abuse (alcohol); suicide.*

 The movie starring Barbra Streisand and Nick Nolte touches on only a few issues from the book. The book is more heartrending and mesmerizing.

For too many years, when we Wingos spoke of our childhood, it seemed a beautiful fantasy. My sister, Savannah, wrote books that sanitized our nightmares. My brother Tom lived life on the edge, perhaps never realizing he was fighting the terrors of his subconscious. As for myself, I preferred to forget the demons of my youth and found solace in forgetfulness. We three had different methods of coping.

I know now our childhood must be faced or it will destroy us. I faced my family history after a single telephone call.

That call informed me that my sister had tried to commit suicide. I must go to New York to face our past so we can live.

Cormier, Robert. **After the First Death.** Pantheon Books, 1979, 237pp.
Grades 9 & Up.

Realistic fiction. *Abuse; crime; death; revenge.*

 All of Robert Cormier's novels are controversial, but they are so well written that you might consider booktalking his books to an older audience.

I have never killed anyone before. This is my first time.

Sure, I've seen Arkin kill, but he's a real pro. This is the first time he has assigned the job to me. At 16, I'm finally old enough to kill.

My assignment is to kill the bus driver. First, I am to wait until the bus is hijacked and the children are given drug-laced candy and become hostages. Then I am to take the bus driver away from the bus to mercifully put a bullet between his eyes.

But, right from the first, things go wrong with our hijacking. First, the bus driver is a girl. How can I murder a young, beautiful girl? The next thing that goes wrong is–.

Look, I don't have time to go into all this, okay? Read *After the First Death* to find out all the rest.

Cormier, Robert. We All Fall Down. Heinmann, 1991, 168pp. Grades 9 & Up.

Realistic fiction. *Crime; illness (mental); love; responsibility; revenge; secrets; trust.*

They entered the house on the evening of April Fool's Day. In the next 45 minutes, four teenagers invaded every room of the house, damaging everything they touched.

It was just bad luck that 14-year-old Karen Jerome arrived at the house during the vandalism. She was found unconscious on the cellar floor.

The Avenger watched it all from his hiding place. It was important to remain hidden. Why? To wait for his revenge. Those animals would be sorry that they had ever thought about trashing his neighbor's house.

So very, very sorry.

Crutcher, Chris. Ironman. GreenWillow, 1995, 181pp. Grades 9 & Up.

Sports. *Men's issues; peer pressure; problem parents; responsibility; school; sports.*

Note: Chris Crutcher's books are usually controversial because of their topics and profanity. If you decide to booktalk his books, you might want to warn others about this in advance.

I plan to be famous one day, just wait and see. I am the future Ironman, also known as Bo Brewster. I am a triathlete—a swimming, bicycling, and running lunatic.

Right now the only thing I'm famous for is my third suspension in school. I don't get it. I'm a nice guy. I don't do drugs, don't cut class–well, hardly ever–rarely fight, and usually turn in my homework.

I've got one major problem: my machine gun mouth. My last suspension was over calling my English teacher a–well, let's just say it's a word that is banned on national television, OK? So suspend me!

Interested? My story will be continued in Chris Crutcher's *Ironman.*

Curwood, James Oliver. Baree: The Story of a Wolf-Dog. Newmarket, 1992, 256pp. First published in 1917. For all ages.

Adventure. *Animals (wolves); ecology; survival.*

Note: James Oliver Curwood's books are good recommendations for admirers of Jack London.

I'm James Oliver Curwood, author of *Baree* as well as other books about animals in the wild. I have 27 guns and I have used them all. I certainly have done my share in contributing to extermination.

However, I want to write stories of wild things as they lived. It is not my desire to humanize them. These animals take life one day at a time, and to survive the day is a victory. Take Baree the wolf-dog, for example. I knew this wolf-dog just as I knew Baree's father. I knew all the animals in this heroic story of an orphaned wolf-pup and his wondrous passage to adulthood.

So, come with me on my journey through the Canadian wilderness. See if you will look at wild animals the same way again.

Delany, Sarah L. & A. Elizabeth, with Amy Hill Hearth. **Having Our Say: The Delany Sisters' First 100 Years.** (Pbk.) Bantam Doubleday Dell, 1993, 299pp. Grades 9 & Up.

Biography. *Aging; African Americans; racism; women's issues.*

I was on assignment for *The New York Times* when I first met the Delany sisters. After my article was published, I received many letters from people who wanted more information about the African-American sisters who were more than 100 years old. Simply put, the public fell in love with these two spirited sisters.

Bessie was the feisty sister. During the days of segregation, she told a white man to shut up and go back to the white folk's section! That remark could have had serious consequences in those days, but Bessie always spoke her mind. Her sister Sadie's way was to "play dumb" and ignore racism.

Their father was a slave who could read and write. At the time reading was against the law for slaves. He encouraged his 10 children to receive an education, and they obeyed. Bessie became a dentist, and Sadie was a teacher.

Bessie and Sadie lived and worked in Harlem during the Renaissance of the 1920s and 1930s. They knew some famous African Americans, including Booker T. Washington, W. E. B. Du Bois, and Paul Robeson.

As I heard their remarkable story, I learned many things about our tainted American past. These Delaney sisters obviously enjoyed having their say.

Doherty, Berlie. **Dear Nobody.** HarperCollins, 1991; (Pbk.) HarperCollins, 1993, 200pp. Grades 9 & Up. A Carnegie Medal winner.

Realistic fiction. *Love; pregnancy; responsibility.*

Note: This award-winning book is about a teenager who finally decides to keep and raise her baby.

Dear Nobody,
Pregnant, pregnant, I may be pregnant.
I've only told Chris. I can't tell anyone else. Not Mom or Ruthlyn.
Go away.
Leave me alone.
I don't want you.
Helen

Dorris, Michael. **A Yellow Raft in Blue Water.** Pan Books, 1988, 343pp. Grades 9 & Up.

Realistic fiction. *African Americans; aging; death; interracial relations; Native Americans; racism; rites of passage.*

Note: The author also tells Rayona's story of her youth in **The Window.** That booktalk is on page 54.

Three generations of Native American women tell their stories of life on a reservation in Montana. Young Rayona, a half-caste with a wandering father, lives with her mother, Christine. Many years ago Christine escaped the reservation for the fast-paced life of Seattle. Christine was raised by the mysterious Aunt Ida, a woman who appeared to have no warmth or kindness.

Each woman tells her side of the family saga. In their telling, they uncover a secret that has slowly eaten into the family fabric.

Draper, Sharon M. **Forged by Fire.**
Atheneum Books for Young People, 1997,
151pp. Grades 9 & Up. A Coretta Scott
King Award winner.

Realistic fiction. *Abuse; African Americans;
eating disorders; sexual abuse; substance
abuse (cocaine and pills).*

 *Sharon Draper also
wrote **Tiger's Don't
Cry,** in which some of
the minor characters from this book
tell their story. That booktalk is on
page 60.*

Do I smell smoke?

Gerald panicked. He began running to his family's three-room apartment. As he ran up the six flights of stairs, he remembered that day long ago behind the couch of his mother's house.

Gerald was only three years old when he played with a cigarette lighter and burned down the house. His mother, Monica, went to jail for child neglect. Gerald lived with his Aunt Queen, a kind woman who gave warm hugs and much praise.

Six years later Monica returned with a new husband and daughter. Gerald loved his half-sister, Angel, immediately, but hated his stepfather on sight. Jacob was abusive to Angel, both physically and sexually. Gerald tried to protect her, but he couldn't always help.

All these thoughts went through Gerald's mind as he ran toward the fire in the apartment. He just hoped and prayed he wasn't too late!

du Maurier, Daphne. **Rebecca.**
Doubleday, 1938, 357pp.; (Pbk.) Avon,
1938, 380pp. Grades 8 & Up.

Mysteries/thrillers. *Great Britain; love;
movie novels; rivalry; secrets.*

Last night I dreamed of Manderly, the stately mansion in which my prosperous husband, Maxim, and I resided many years ago. We can never go back to Manderly. Rebecca and her housekeeper, Mrs. Danvers, have seen to that.

The ghost of Rebecca has haunted my life. Rebecca was Maxim's first wife, who died in a dreadful drowning accident on the estate. Her presence surrounded our marriage and the property. When I arrived, all I heard was how beautiful and charming Rebecca was, until she seemed as real as Mrs. Danvers.

Her ghostly presence was ruining my marriage with Maxim. Something was troubling him. Was it his sorrow over losing Rebecca?

Mrs. Danvers hated me because she thought I was trying to replace Rebecca. Did she have secrets about Rebecca that she was hiding?

I have learned many secrets about the mysterious Rebecca. I will tell you all I know.

Duncan, Lois. **Who Killed my Daughter?** Delacorte, 1992, 289pp. Grades 7 & Up. A Senior Readers' Choice Award winner.

Nonfiction. *Crime; death; occult; substance abuse; supernatural.*

 Note: Also, mention that Kait's story was on the television show **Unsolved Mysteries,** and that the Duncan family has a Web site asking for help in solving the mystery.

On the night of July 16, 1989, while driving alone in her car in Albuquerque, New Mexico, Kaitlyn Arquette was shot twice in the head. Only 18, she died the next morning. The murder has never been solved.

Kaitlyn's mother is Lois Duncan, a young adult suspense writer. What is eerie is that Duncan's books forecast Kaitlyn's murder.

For example, in the book *Summer of Fear*, one of the characters is named Mike Gallagher; later, Mike Gallagher becomes a real-life detective in Kait's murder. In the book *The Third Eye*, Anne Summers is a psychic detective; later, the real-life psychic detective bears an extraordinary resemblance to the character. In *Don't Look Behind You*, published two months before Kait's murder, the main character, April, is stalked by a man in a Camaro, similar to the car Kait was driving when she was murdered. The stalker's name in the book is Mike Vamp; the alleged murderer of Kait is named Mike Vamp!

Read this tragic true story. Then try reading suspense books by Lois Duncan. You will find some amazing similarities between fact and fiction.

Dyer, Daniel. **Jack London: A Biography.** Scholastic, 1997, 221pp. Grades 8 & Up.

Biography. *Men's issues; substance abuse (alcohol); work.*

Some people think Jack London's life was his best story. In 1904 Jack London was one of the most famous, well-paid authors in the world. His books *The Call of the Wild* and *White Fang* were widely read.

Yet a decade earlier Jack London, also known as John Lundon, was arrested for vagrancy and served 30 days of hard labor in prison. He had also been a pirate, a seal hunter, a mill worker, a Klondike gold miner, a hobo, and a political activist.

As a boy Jack grew up fast. He got drunk for the first time at five years old. At 10 he left school to begin earning a living for his family. At 19 he reentered school as a ninth grader so he could make a living by using his brains rather than his brawn. By 20 he was enrolled in college.

Dead at 40, Jack London had lived a life of two men. See why his own life is Jack London's best story.

de Saint Exupery, Antoine. **The Little Prince.** Translated from the French by Katherine Woods. Harcourt, Brace, Jovanovich, 1971, 111pp. First published in 1943. For all ages.

Fantasy. *Death; ethics; magic; movie novels; work.*

> **Note:** If the audience is curious about the secret, you can tell them the secret is "What is essential is invisible and can only be seen with the heart." I also explain that this book is similar to **Animal Farm** in that both are analogies. Both are deceptively simple in structure.

What is the secret of happiness?

The little prince lived all alone on a small planet no bigger than a house. He traveled from planet to planet, meeting a king, a conceited man, an alcoholic, a businessman, and a streetlamp-lighter. Each one of them was very strange to the little prince, except for the lamplighter, who at least had a job that thought of others.

Eventually the little prince landed on Earth and met a fox. The fox was the wisest of them all. He was the creature who explained the secret of happiness to the little prince.

Giblin, James Cross. **Charles A. Lindbergh: A Human Hero.** Clarion Books, 1997, 212pp. For all ages.

Biography. *Europe (France); love; work.*

In the 1920s Charles Lindbergh was the most famous person in America, as famous as John Glenn is today. There was no television, but there were newspapers and radios. The media obsessively reported Lindbergh's solo airplane flight across the Atlantic, the kidnapping and death of his son, and his conservative politics.

Who was the real Lindbergh? This courageous man had achieved his dreams as a pilot almost entirely on his own. He began his flying career by "barnstorming"–walking outside an aircraft on the lower wing. Later he perfected a double parachute jump by cutting off the first parachute to free fall before pulling his second chute.

His airplane flight in *The Spirit of Saint Louis* was especially remarkable because he helped design the plane, secured the funds and flew a solo round trip across the Atlantic. He was only 25 years old!

When his infant son was kidnapped in 1930, Charles Lindbergh became the first tabloid celebrity. The alleged kidnapper was tried in the "trial of the century" and then executed.

Later his public appeal declined when he flew to Nazi Germany and publicly endorsed their government.

Who was Charles Lindbergh? He was a human hero, capable of great deeds and flawed by weaknesses. Just like you and me.

Gordeeva, Ekaterina, with E. M. Swift. **My Sergei: A Love Story.** (Pbk.) Mass Market, 1997, 340pp. Grades 8 & Up.

Biography. *Death; love; movie novels; Russia; sex and sexuality; sports (ice skating); work.*

I consider myself an ice skater first, then a woman, then a mother. I wish I wasn't this way. Maybe this was the reason Sergei came into my life. Maybe he was there to teach me to share more of my feelings off the ice.

I'm Ekaterina Gordeeva. My husband, Sergei Grinkov, and I won two Olympic gold medals, four world championships, and the adoration of millions. Suddenly, on November 20, 1995, my Sergei died of a heart attack, leaving me with my young daughter, Daria. He was only 28.

I want Sergei to know I will always take good care of our daughter. I want her to know the kind of man he was. That's why I'm writing this memoir, before the lovely echo fades, as it will with time.

I want to share my Sergei with you, too.

Grant, Cynthia D. **Mary Wolf.** Atheneum, 1995, 166pp. Grades 9 & Up.

Realistic fiction. *Abuse; crime; death; problem parents; sexual abuse; substance abuse (alcohol).*

 This book is well written but disturbing because Mary Wolf kills her father.

Mary Wolf can't help her feelings. She is embarrassed by her family. Her dad can't keep a job. Her mom regularly shoplifts from stores. Her younger sisters are always wearing old and tattered clothes. Her family doesn't really have a home except for the van where they live and sleep. Now Mary's mom is pregnant again! Mary is just too mortified for words.

Mary Wolf didn't know that these feelings were churning within her like a pressure cooker. One day these feelings would explode and lead to a disaster that Mary would have to endure for the rest of her life.

Griffin, John Howard. **Black Like Me.** Signet, 1977, 192pp. Updated with a new epilogue. Grades 9 & Up.

Biography. *African Americans; interracial relations; racism; secrets.*

What would it be like to change your race?

John Howard Griffin did just that. In 1959 he began taking prescribed medication to darken his skin. Then he began his journey through the segregated Southern states to personally experience what it would be like to be an African American.

Here is his story.

I suggest that you keep this booktalk short and simple because the topic will sell itself. Sometimes I tell people that in the 1990s a college student tried the same experiment and was so distressed by the reactions from people that, after two weeks, he ended his experiment.

Guy, Rosa. **The Music of Summer.**
Delacorte, 1992, 180pp. Grades 9 & Up.

Romance. *African Americans; love; revenge; rivalry; sex and sexuality.*

 Author Rosa Guy is described in Mayo Angelou's autobiographical book **The Heart of a Woman.** *You might booktalk Rosa Guy's books and then booktalk Maya Angelou's book on page 102.*

At 18, Sarah Richardson had it all: beauty, talent, the love of her family. Maybe that's why her so-called friend Cathy hated her.

Sarah had only an inkling of her friend's hatred, but Cathy's true feelings were soon obvious. Sarah invited herself along with Cathy's family to Cape Cod for the summer. Cathy encouraged her friends to taunt and tease Sarah over her dark color and any other little thing. Sarah was just about ready to terminate the friendship and go home.

Then Jean Pierre Arman arrived from Africa with his mother for a visit. Tall, dark, and handsome, almost 30 and available, Jean Pierre fell for Sarah. He wanted to marry her and take her back to Africa with him.

Sarah had already accepted that Cathy hated her. She had no idea that this love affair would enrage Cathy so much that she would try to commit murder!

Hahn, Mary Downing. **The Wind Blows Backward.** Clarion, 1993, 263pp. Grades 9 & Up. An ALA Best Books for Young Adults selection.

Romance. *Death; illness (mental); love; sex and sexuality; suicide.*

 This is recommended for mature teenagers, due to its sexual content.

Casey and I call Spencer Adams the Prince of Jocks. Spencer is handsome, popular, and a star athlete. Many years ago I even called him a friend until he ended our friendship to move into a faster and more sophisticated crowd. He even stopped speaking to me, although he never mocks me as his crowd does.

One day Spencer makes contact. He asks me out for a date and confides some troubling secrets about himself and his so-called perfect family. As we fall in love, I learn that Spencer is even thinking of suicide.

How can I help Spencer help himself?

Heinlein, Robert A. **Stranger in a Strange Land.** G. P. Putnam's Sons, 1987, 438pp. First published in 1961. Grades 9 & Up.

Science fiction. *Death; love; politics; religion; science.*

 This classic novel is much more than a romance. Eventually Smith creates a religious cult with a philosophy that is similar to New Age philosophy. The ending is a shocker. Interestingly, this book was banned at the time of publication, but quickly became an underground classic.

Once upon a future time, there was a Martian named Valentine Michael Smith.

Smith had the ancestry of a Human, but thought and acted like a Martian. How's that, you ask? Smith had Earth parents who landed and perished on Mars. Smith was adopted by the Martians and was taught grokking and water-sharing. When Smith was brought to Earth, he became a stranger in a strange land. Smith didn't even know what a woman was or did.

Then Smith met Jill Boardman, a supervisory nurse on the hospital floor where he lived. They were fascinated by each other. Smith even allowed Jill to kidnap him so he would not be forced to sign papers giving away the inheritance his parents left him.

How will Jill manage to protect this alien? How will Jill manage not to fall in love with this stranger in a strange land?

Hemingway, Ernest. **The Old Man and the Sea.** Charles Scribner's Sons, 1952, 127pp. Grades 8 & Up.

Adventure. *Aging; death; ecology; men's issues; movie novels; sports; survival.*

 *Reluctant readers enjoy Hemingway's deceptively simple style.*

Anyone can be a fisherman in May. In September fishing is an art.

The old man knows he was born for fishing. Just as Joe DiMaggio was born for baseball, the old man was born for fishing. The young boy knows it, too.

On that special September day the old man wishes the young boy was with him to help him capture the biggest fish he had ever seen. Instead it is just the old man. Alone. The old man, the fish, and the sea, trapped in a battle for life.

What is this? The old man is not alone after all. Are those hungry sharks surrounding the old man in the sea?

Henderson, David. **'Scuse Me While I Kiss the Sky.** Bantam, 1983, 411pp. First published in 1978. Grades 9 & Up.

Biography. *African Americans; music; sex and sexuality; show business; substance (alcohol and drugs).*

The world's greatest guitar player never had a music lesson. Jimi Hendrix learned to play by practice, practice, practice. When Jimi joined the Screaming Eagles Paratroopers, he liked to jump from airplanes and hear the sound of wind, of engines, of air. He learned to imitate these sounds on the guitar. Eventually he began sleeping with his guitar, talking to it, and calling it by name after painting "Betty Jane" on it. People began to call Jimi Hendrix crazy.

Jimi wasn't crazy. He was motivated to be the best. He started out playing with Little Richard, the Monkees, and Ike and Tina Turner. As an attraction he played the guitar with his teeth. Once or twice he set his guitar on fire!

Jimi once said, "When I die, I want people to play my music, go wild and freak out and do anything they want to do." This musical genius lived only 27 years. Even his death in London in 1970 was controversial. Find out why.

Huxley, Aldous. **Brave New World.** HarperPerennial, 1932, 269pp. Foreword by author written in 1946. Grades 9 & Up.

Science fiction. *Class conflict; politics; religion; sex and sexuality; substance abuse.*

For readers that loved **The Giver** *by Lois Lowry, this book is an excellent choice. This book is also reminiscent of* **Stranger in a Strange Land,** *by Robert Heinlein, and of* **1984,** *by George Orwell.*

Six hundred years into our future lies a brave new world. No books. No flowers. No parents. No love.

Our Ford was the first to reveal the dangers of family life. With mothers and fathers having so many temptations and prohibitions, parents were forced to feel strongly. No wonder humans were once so unstable! Our Ford promised happiness if all thoughts of family were abolished forever.

Bernard Marx was curious about the days Before Ford. He visited the New Mexico Reservation of Savages. On the reservation Savages maintained the ancient customs of marriage, family, and religion.

Bernard also met Linda and her son, John. Many years ago Linda was exiled to the Reservation when she gave birth to John. Now Bernard wanted to take these Savages back to civilization with him.

Will these Savages survive in this brave new world?

Ji Li Jiang. **Red Scarf Girl: A Memoir of the Cultural Revolution.** Foreword by David Henry Hwang. HarperCollins, 1997, 285pp.; (Pbk.) HarperTrophy, 1998, 285pp. For all ages.

Biography. *China; class conflict; peer pressure; politics; responsibility.*

 *This book is difficult to categorize, but is a must read.*

In 1966 the Cultural Revolution began.

That year I was 12 years old and living in Communist China under the leadership of the great Mao Ze-dong. That year I became a red scarf girl.

Part of the Cultural Revolution was to banish the *Four Olds*: old ideas, old culture, old customs, old habits. It even became a crime to respect our elders, such as parents and teachers. Did they really intend to ruin our health and corrupt our minds? If so, why hadn't we noticed?

One day my name was slandered, as well. The propaganda newsletter said I was a teacher's favorite because I was rich, not because I was clever. My fellow students sneered at my family's background because my grandfather was a landlord.

How could I suddenly turn from good to bad? Why should I be ashamed of my family and myself?

Kerr, M. E. **Deliver Us from Evie.** (Pbk.) HarperTrophy, 1994, 177pp. Grades 9 & Up.

Realistic fiction. *Homosexuality; sex and sexuality.*

"Hey, we know about your brother! What's his name again?"
"Doug Burrman," I said.
"Nah, not that brother. Your other brother."
"I only have one brother," I said.
"What about Evie?"

Yeah, what about Evie? I guess my sister doesn't really fit in this hick farming community with her slicked-back hair, bomber jacket, and masculine stride. Now that she's going out with Patsy Duff, the whole town is talking.

Okay, I helped put up the sign over the memorial statue that read, "Evie loves Patsy and vice versa!" I thought that would snap Evie out of this infatuation. Little did I know the trouble that sign would cause!

Klause, Annette Curtis. **Blood and Chocolate.** Delacorte, 1997, 267pp. Grades 9 & Up. An ALA Best Books for Young Adults selection.

Horror. *Love; occult; secrets; supernatural.*

He knows, thought Vivien. This guy named Aiden Teague knows what I am.

Vivien loved to paint, especially vivid pictures of the mysterious moon. Her art teacher raved about her powers of expression and recommended that Vivien's artwork be published in the school literary magazine. In the magazine next to Vivien's artwork was a poem "Wolf Changes." It was written by another student, Aiden Teague.

After meeting him, Vivien found herself attracted to this meat boy. As they begin to date, Vivian knew there would be trouble. Hadn't her mother warned her not to play with her food?

You guessed it. Vivian is a werewolf. Should she bare her claws and tell all to Aiden?

Koertge, Ron. The Arizona Kid. (Pbk.) Avon Flare, 1989, 215pp. Grades 9 & Up.

Realistic fiction. *AIDS; homosexuality; men's issues; sex and sexuality; substance abuse.*

Yippie ti yi yay! I'm in the West! The Wild West!

Sorry. I'll try to be cool, but it's hard when I think about spending a summer away from my parents–whom I love, but, let's face it, parents are parents. I'll bet the girls are as hot as the Arizona weather. I mean to learn me a few things about girls while I'm out here staying with my Uncle Wes.

Uncle Wes isn't into girls at all. I wonder what that's like. I mean, how can Uncle Wes not see the appeal of Cara Mae. She is nothing like the girls back home. Yep, our summer romance on a dude ranch is just perfect for someone like me.

Just call me the Arizona Kid.

Krakauer, Jon. Into the Wild. Villard Books, 1996, 207pp.; (Pbk.) Anchor/Doubleday, 1997, 206pp. Grades 9 & Up.

Adventure. *Class conflict; death; men's issues; responsibility; rites of passage; runaways; secrets; survival.*

On September 6, 1992, a decomposed body was discovered inside an old bus that sits inside the Delani National Park in Alaska. Outside the bus was an SOS letter asking for help. The man's body weighed only 67 pounds; he had obviously died of starvation.

Who was this man? He was Christopher Johnson McCandless, from a well-to-do East Coast family. Chris had just graduated with honors from Emory University. After graduation he changed his name to Alexander Supertramp. Ironically, considering his death by starvation, he gave his entire balance of $24,000 to a charity for the hungry.

Then Alex Supertramp began his journey across the States that would eventually claim his life . . .

Le Guin, Ursula K. A Wizard of Earthsea. Illustrated by Ruth Robbins. Parnassus Press, 1968, 183pp. Grades 8 & Up. First in a series: **The Tombs of Atuan; The Farthest Shore;** and **Tehanu** follow.

Fantasy. *End-of-the-world; magic; occult; rites of passage; supernatural.*

Long ago in the magical islands of Earthsea lived the greatest wizard of them all: Sparrowhawk, also known as Ged. His life is told in the Deed of Ged, but this is a tale of the time before his fame.

As a young boy Ged was taught his skills by a peasant witch. Ged was responsible for bringing on the thick, white fog that protected the villagers from an attack by the deadly Kargs. Through this act, he was taught more wizardry by Ogion the Silent. Ogion warned Ged that every word, every act of their Art was said and done either for good or evil. However, Ged longed for glory and ignored his teacher's warnings.

Yes, Ged's power was magnificent and much admired by all. Unfortunately, Ged was boastful and arrogant. Little did he know he needed all his self control to fight the most deadly and dangerous force of them all–himself.

Lee, Harper. **To Kill a Mockingbird.**
(Pbk.) Warner Books, 1960, 281pp.
Grades 9 & Up.

Historical fiction. *African Americans;
illness (mental); interracial relations;
movie novels; racism; rites of passage;
sexual abuse.*

Jem and I sometimes discussed the events leading to his accident. I said the Ewells started it all, but Jem claimed it started long before that. He said it began the summer we met Dill and when he first gave us the idea of making Boo Radley come out.

The Radley Place fascinated Dill. We were told Boo was inside the house, but no one had ever seen him. Folks said he was crazy, that he went out nights and peered through windows. It was said all small crimes in the area were Boo's work.

However, nobody said Boo was responsible for attacking Mayella Ewell; she said it was Tom Robinson, a local "colored" man. This ugly incident was the talk of the town. We were thrown in the middle of it since our Dad, Atticus, was Tom Robinson's defending attorney.

How did all these people cause Jem's accident? Well, it's a long story. You better start at the beginning of my book so I can tell it nice and proper.

Lester, Julius. **To Be a Slave.**
Illustrated by Tom Feelings. Dial Books
for Young Readers, 1968, 160pp.
Grades 9 & Up. A Newbery Honor book.

Nonfiction. *Abuse; African Americans;
racism; runaways; sexual abuse.*

What would it be like to be a slave? The only way we would know is to be a slave or to talk to someone who has been a slave. Julius Lester accomplished this difficult task by going to the archives of the Library of Congress, Fisk University, and other sources.

First, how were the Africans captured to become slaves? Slave traders would place pieces of red cloth in a trail to lure Africans onto the ships. The Africans were attracted to the bright color and followed the trail, only to be kidnapped and taken to America in chains. Sometimes African chiefs sold their prisoners to slave traders. Most were individually kidnapped.

If these Africans survived the horrendous Middle Passage of the ships, they were sold on the auction block and led away to a life of servitude. Many were beaten. Most were subjected to hard labor and sexual abuse. All lost their family, country, language, and name.

Here are their stories, told by the people who experienced

London, Jack. **The Call of the Wild.**
(Pbk.) Classic Pocket, 1974, 102pp.
First published in 1903. For all ages.

Adventure. *Animals (wild dogs); rivalry;
survival.*

 *This classic story
appeals to all ages, and
is especially appealing
to those readers who love animals.*

Buck never knew he became a legend in the harsh and frozen Yukon during the Klondike Rush. The Yeehat tribe called Buck *Ghost Dog* because he was the cleverest of all the wild dogs that roamed the Yukon. Buck knew nothing of this. All Buck instinctively knew was that he wanted to survive any way he could.

Buck learned how to survive harsh weather, beatings, starvation and many traumas. Born in luxury, Buck didn't know he had survival skills until he was forced to use them. Sold as a sledge dog, Buck learned how to lead a dog team through blizzards and across icy rivers. Later this proud dog escaped captivity to become the leader of a wolf-pack and a legend in his time.

Lord, Walter. **A Night to Remember.**
(Pbk.) Bantam, 1997, 209pp. First
published in 1955. Grades 7 & Up.

Nonfiction. *Class conflict; death; movie
novels; survival.*

The Titanic was a miracle of 20th-century technology. Yet one moonlit night in April 1912, the Titanic hit an iceberg and sank. Only 20 lifeboats were on board for 2,207 passengers.

That night brought out the best and worst of human nature. Women and children were placed on lifeboats first. The men followed if there was room. Some wives refused to go without their husbands. One man put on a shawl and tried to disguise himself as a woman. Some men wore full evening dress to their watery deaths. As the ship sank, the musicians continued playing the Episcopal hymn "Autumn." The total number of lives lost was estimated at 1,502.

The sinking of the Titanic was a night to remember–forever.

Lovell, Jim, & Jeffrey Kluger. **Apollo 13.**
(Pbk.) Pocket Books, 1994, 418pp.
Grades 8 & Up. Previously titled **Lost
Moon.**

Biography. *Movie novels; science;
survival; work.*

Nobody knew how the stories about the poison pills started. Most people had heard them. Some even believed them. The press and the public certainly did. Even some people at the Agency believed the stories.

Stories about the poison pills always made astronaut Jim Lovell laugh. Poison pills! Forget it! There just wasn't any situation in which you'd ever consider making an early exit.

However, if there was a time Jim Lovell, Fred Haise, and Jack Swigert might have considered poison pills, it was during a flight to the moon in 1970. Everything on Apollo 13 went wrong. There was an explosion, a shortage of power and oxygen, and a typhoon warning during descent.

Who had the time to think of suicide during a time like this? They were too busy trying to survive!

Lovell, Mary. **The Sound of Wings: The Life of Amelia Earhart.** St. Martin's Press, 1989, 420pp. Grades 9 & Up.

Biography. *Problem parents; responsibility; substance abuse (alcohol); work; women's issues.*

When Amelia Earhart mysteriously disappeared in 1939, she was known as the greatest female aviator. Who was she really?

The public had no idea that Amelia had suffered several crashes due to her technical errors. She couldn't read radio signals, even though she planned an around-the-world trip that might require such a skill. She knowingly hired a navigator for this dangerous trip who was an alcoholic.

What made Amelia Earhart take chances without being fully prepared?

Lyons, Mary E. **Keeping Secrets: The Girlhood Diaries of Seven Women Writers.** Henry Holt, 1995, 232pp. Grades 9 & Up.

Biography. *Diaries; interracial relations; love; work; women's issues.*

A diary is the perfect friend for keeping secrets–until it's read.

A diary can also become a historical record of how people lived. In the 19th century, keeping a diary was the only way some women could express their innermost thoughts and dreams.

Louisa May Alcott requested that all her diaries be burned at her death, but some survived. Some revealing secrets were discovered. For instance, she hated writing *Little Women*. In her diary she complained that she "never liked girls or knew many, except my sisters." Instead, she loved writing about topics such as incest, drug abuse, suicide, and mind control. She used the pen name A. M. Barnard for all her thriller novels. This secret was uncovered in 1943!

Sarah Jane Parker, a white, Northern schoolteacher, fell in love with one of her pupils, a freed slave. Her diary reveals more about her feelings than Sarah would or could admit publicly.

All of the seven fascinating women discussed in this book will unlock the keys of their diaries and admit you into their souls.

McBride, James. **The Color of Water: A Black Man's Tribute to His White Mother.** Riverhead Books, 1996, 228pp.; (Pbk.) Riverhead Books, 1998, 232pp. Grades 8 & Up.

Biography. *African Americans; interracial relations; racism.*

"What color is God?" I asked my mother.

"God is the color of water. Water doesn't have a color," my mother answered.

In the real world, my mother was "Mrs. McBride" or "Mrs. Jordan," depending on whether she used my father or stepfather's name. In church she was "Sister Jordan."

Sister Jordan was quite a woman. She was from an orthodox Jewish family, became a born-again Christian, married two black men, and was a mother to 12 children. Quite a woman.

When I was younger, I was ashamed of my mother. I didn't want the world to know I had a white mother. Now as a grown man, I feel privileged.

It is my honor to present to you, Mrs. McBride, Mrs. Jordan, Sister Jordan–my mother.

McCullers, Carson. **The Member of the Wedding.** Bantam, 1958, 153pp. First published in 1946. Grades 8 & Up.

Historical fiction. *African Americans; death; interracial relations; movie novels; rites of passage.*

Frankie Addams is 12 years old and she is afraid. She is five-foot-three and wears a size seven shoe. She had grown four inches this year! At the rate of four inches a year, she will soon be over six feet tall–a freak, like those freaks she saw once in the circus.

Frankie hates her body and her thoughts, which she knows are wicked and mean. She can't seem to stop herself from being a lazy loafer who hangs around the kitchen, taunting and teasing her housekeeper, Bernice, and her five-year-old neighbor, John Henry.

Frankie had not always been this way. Before the summer she felt normal and unafraid. She had many friends and had liked herself.

The only good thing about this dreadful summer is that her brother is getting married. Frankie hopes this will make a difference in her life. Just how, she isn't certain, but it just has to. Being a member of the wedding would show everyone she belongs–no matter how she feels inside.

Martinez, Victor. **Parrot in the Oven.** HarperCollins, 1996, 216pp. Grades 8 & Up. A National Book Award winner.

Realistic fiction. *Hispanic Americans; men's issues; self-identity; sex and sexuality.*

Perico or parrot is what Dad calls me sometimes. It is from a Mexican saying about a parrot who complains how hot it is in the shade, when all along he is sitting inside an oven. People usually say this about ignorant people. I think Dad doesn't think I'm ignorant, just too trusting. He thinks I would go right into the oven trusting people.

Maybe he's right. I do think one day my dad's drinking will stop and that he will find a job. One day my mom will stop cleaning our spotless house in the projects and spend time with us. One day my older brother, Nardo, will stop flipping through jobs like a thumb through a deck of cards. One day my older sister, Magda, will quite sneaking out of the house to date one of her lovers.

One day I'll come home to find everything just as I dreamed it.

Miklowitz, Gloria D. **Past Forgiving.** Simon & Schuster Books for Young People, 1995, 153pp. Grades 8 & Up.

Realistic fiction. *Love; men's issues; sex and sexuality; sexual abuse; women's issues.*

Note: *This book is about physical abuse and date rape.*

Cliff is everything I've ever wanted in a guy. He's handsome, popular, athletic, and madly in love with me. That's why he acts so crazy sometimes. He loves me so much that he doesn't want me confiding in my best friend, Jenna, or talking to Brian, the head camp counselor. He wants me all to himself. Isn't that sweet?

Sometimes Cliff loses control. Once or twice he even hit me, leaving me with dark purple bruises. Of course, he always apologizes and tells me that he's afraid of losing me. One night he got so mad that . . .

Never mind. I only told Jenna. Jenna was horrified and wanted me to call the police.

What happens when apologies aren't enough? What happens when I am past forgiving?

Mitchell, Margaret. **Gone with the Wind.** Warner Books, 1964, 1024pp. First published in 1936. Grades 9 & Up.

Historical fiction. *Civil War; interracial relations; love; movie novels; survival.*

 Try this one in your best Southern belle accent.

"Cathleen," whispered 17-year-old Scarlett O'Hara during rest time at the Wilkes' barbecue. "Who is that nasty man downstairs named Butler?"

"My dear, don't you know? He has the most terrible reputation. His name is Rhett Butler. Even his own parents don't speak to him. He took this girl out buggy riding until morning and then refused to marry her! Then he had a duel with the girl's brother and killed him!"

Scarlett had no way of knowing that this rascal would reappear in her life like her recurring nightmare about running through a misty fog. Her tumultuous relationship with Rhett Butler lasted through the Civil War, two husbands, three children, and many adventures. Unfortunately, Scarlett is convinced she is in love with Ashley Wilkes, her sister-in-law's husband. She couldn't love two men at the same time, could she?

"Oh, fiddle-dee-dee," thought Scarlett. "I'll worry about that tomorrow."

Montgomery, L. M. **Anne of Green Gables.** With an afterward by Mary Rubio & Elizabeth Waterson. Penguin Books. 1987, 317pp. For all ages.

Historical fiction. Adoption; movie novels; orphans; rites of passage.

"I'm not expecting a girl from the orphan asylum. I'm here to pick up a boy to help me on the farm." That mouthful was the most that shy Matthew Cuthbert of Green Gables had said in years.

Still, there was no boy waiting at the train station. Instead, a red-headed girl in an ugly gray dress and sailor hat cheerfully introduced herself. Anne Shirley was 11 years old and so talkative that Matthew didn't have to think about his fear of little girls. She captured tongued-tied Matthew's heart immediately.

His sister, Marilla, was not so sold on Anne. She rightfully recognized that Anne would be a handful.

Anne's impulsive character would land her in many scrapes. Once she tried to dye her red hair and turned it green! Another time Gilbert Blythe called her "Carrots." She slammed her school slate over his head and cracked it–the slate, not his head. When Mrs. Rachel Lynde called Anne "skinny and ugly," she called Mrs. Lynde "fat and clumsy."

However, Anne is lovable in spite of her faults. That's why this series has been in print since 1908 with translations all over the world. Travel to Avonlea with Anne of Green Gables.

Napoli, Donna Jo. **The Magic Circle.** Dutton, 1993, 118pp. Grades 9 & Up.

Folklore. *Aging; magic; occult; revenge; supernatural.*

 This book contains images of witchcraft that might disturb a younger reader. However, an older, reluctant reader or a young, mature reader might enjoy this brief and well-written novel.

I am a witch. You might have heard of me. I am the witch who tempted Hansel and Gretel into my tantalizing gingerbread house. Instead of eating the children, I was pushed into the oven and destroyed forever.

I was not always an evil witch. True, I was always ugly, but I did not work for the devils. I was once a sorceress. The devils worked for me. One day the devils tricked me while I was performing a healing inside the magic circle, and I became the wicked witch you now see.

Come with me into the magic circle and I will tell you my tragic story.

Nelson, Theresa. **Earthshine.** Orchard Books. 1994, 182pp. Grades 9 & Up. An ALA Best Books for Young Adults selection.

Realistic fiction. *AIDS; death; homosexuality; illness (physical).*

 This book is unforgettable. Don't miss this one.

My dad has AIDS. He got it before anyone knew what it was, and now he's dying a little bit every day. You've just got to meet my dad before he–well, you've just got to meet my dad, that's all. A lively, spirited, humorous imp, that's my dad. Everyone loves him. You will, too.

I'm Slim and I live with my dad and his friend, Larry. We take life a day at a time. We enjoy the good times, like when Larry bought my dad a ridiculous wig that made him look like a poodle. We treasure the bad times, too, like when I told Larry I wished he had the disease instead of my dad.

You see, each day that my dad is alive is a special day for us.

Orwell, George. **Animal Farm: A Fairy Story.** Penguin Books, 1945, 95pp. Grades 7 & Up.

Fantasy. *Aging; animals; class conflict; Great Britain; politics; rivalry; work.*

 I tell students that this is an analogy of the Russian Revolution of 1917, but they can read it as a fable if they like. I also recommend Orwell's companion book **1984,** a title that confuses students. I explain that Orwell wrote it in 1948 as a futuristic novel, never realizing that his book would endure past the year 1984.

The revolution has begun!

Animal Farm is the new name of *Manor Farm.* The animals have deposed the owner, Mr. Jones, and assumed ownership. No more late feedings, no more backbreaking work, and no more being sent to the glue factory at an old age.

Of course, as in all revolutions, things are a bit disorderly at first. Who will be the leader? Will it be Napoleon or Snowball? All the pigs seem to be natural leaders, so what other animals will do the hard labor? Who will write the laws? Who will sing the rebellion song, "Beasts of England"? There are so many problems, with so little time to solve them.

All animals agree that anything on two legs is an enemy. Whatever goes upon four legs, or has wings, is a friend. All animals are equal. These rules are part of the Seven Commandments placed on the barn for all animals to read–those animals who can read.

So why do pigs sleep in the big house? Why do pigs command the killer dogs to attack those who oppose their ideas? Just what is happening on Animal Farm?

Peck, Robert Newton. **A Day No Pigs Would Die.** Dell, 1977, 139pp. For all ages.

Historical fiction. *Death; ethics; illness (physical); religion; religious prejudice; rites of passage; work.*

 *This classic can be taught on just about any level or can be added to any reading lists.*

Reckon my life might be different from your'n. Me, I'm a Shaker in Vermont. My pa kills pigs for a living. My ma says he smells of honest work. He can't read, write, or vote, but I reckon he's as good a man as ever walked the earth. He teaches me as good as any teacher–about working hard, doing the right thing, and dying with courage.

Speaking of teachers, Aunty Matty once tried to learn me grammar. A "tutor" she calls herself. The only "tutor" I knowed was a coronet Jacob Henry played in the school band. Sounded like fun 'til Aunty Matty commenced to diagramming sentences, drawing ovals and squiggles all over the paper. The worse it looked, the better she liked it. I thanked her nice and proper for her tutoring, though it shore didn't make any musical noise. Aunty Matty told Ma next time she would teach a pig.

Pullman, Philip. **The Broken Bridge.** Random House, 1990, 218pp. Grades 8 & Up.

Realistic fiction. *Homosexuality; interracial relations; problem parents; racism; secrets; self-identity; sex and sexuality; trust.*

 Philip Pullman will probably be one of the young adult writers that endures. This one is for mature audiences because the main character discovers her best male friend is gay–another lie and secret she must accept.

Secrets and lies, lies and secrets. It's enough to drive me crazy. First, I have a black mother from Haiti. I think she's dead, and now I find out, she's alive. Next, I have no brothers or sisters. Then this half-brother pops up in my life. Then my father might have been in jail. On and on and on . . .

I feel like the broken bridge that is in the small Welsh town where I live. Can I ever find out the truth so I can find who I am?

Pullman, Philip. **The Golden Compass.** Also published under the title **Northern Lights.** With an introduction by Terry Brooks. Alfred A. Knopf, 1995, 399pp. Grades 9 & Up. First in the *Dark Materials* series: **The Subtle Knife** follows. The trilogy will be completed shortly.

Fantasy. *End-of-the-world; magic; occult; supernatural; survival.*

 Due to the enthusiastic approval of fantasy writers like Terry Brooks, this book became an instant classic among fantasy lovers.

One afternoon Lyra and her daemon–disguised as a moth–hide in the Retiring Room of the Master of Jordan College. When Lyra sees the Master put poison into a wineglass, she knows she has stumbled onto a sinister plot. It appears that the Master plans to murder Lyra's uncle, Lord Asreil!

Lyra warns her uncle about the poisoned wineglass, just in time. In exchange, he tells her of the magic dust that is found only in the Arctic North. This dust can unite whole universes. There are those (like the Master) who fear the dust and will do anything to destroy it–even commit murder!

That information leads Lyra and her daemon on a perilous journey. They set out to the Far North to locate the magic dust.

Can they save the universe before it's too late?

Rana, Indi. **The Roller Birds of Rampur.** Henry Holt, 1993, 298pp. Grades 9 & Up.

Realistic fiction. *India and Pakistan; religion; religious prejudice; self-identity; women's issues.*

 Note: This thought-provoking and well-written book gives a detailed account of India's philosophy, religion, and culture through Sheila's grandfather. A mature reader will be fascinated by the characters and events that occur, but a reluctant reader may find this book "boring."

The first words my boyfriend's mother said when she met me were, "Sheila? I thought Sheila was an English name."

Those words would haunt me. You see, I'm not English. I'm from India, but now I reside in England. I'm sure my heritage was the reason I never saw my boyfriend or his mother again.

Who am I? Certainly not English, definitely not a traditional Indian. Where do I fit? Perhaps my trip back to India will bring me the answers I so desperately need.

Rhue, Morton. **The Wave.** (Pbk.) Penguin, 1981, 107pp. Grades 6 & Up.

Realistic fiction. *Peer pressure; religious prejudice; responsibility; school.*

 Note: This book provokes fascinating discussions about mind control.

The Wave is sweeping throughout the school. The Wave is out of control. What began as an experiment has turned into a fanatic cult.

This true story occurred in a high school history class in Palo Alto, California, in 1969. Teacher Ron Jones called The Wave "one of the most frightening events I have ever witnessed in a classroom."

How can The Wave be stopped?

Sagan, Carl. **Contact.** (Pbk.) Pocket Books, 1997, 434pp. Grades 9 & Up.

Science Fiction. *Death; movie novels; science; time travel; women's issues; work.*

 Note: Scientist Carl Sagan's book is more scientifically detailed and complex than the movie.

Flash! Flash! A signal from outer space!

Ellie Arroway is a respected scientist. Like most scientists, she is skeptical of anything that can't be explained. She doesn't necessarily believe in God, extraterrestrials, or time travel. She also knows as a scientist that she has to keep an open mind.

However, when Ellie discovers a message in prime numbers from the star Vega, she knows she must contact the President of the United States. Soon Earth's scientists begin to decode the cryptic message.

Who—and what—is out there?

Schreiber, Flora Rheta. **Sybil.** Warner Books, 1973, 460pp. Grades 9 & Up.

Biography. *Abuse; illness (mental); movie novels; sexual abuse.*

Five days lost.

Sybil Isabel Dorsett glanced at a newspaper and panicked. Where had the time gone? Where had she been?

In her small, rented room Sybil discovered rumpled pajamas she had never seen before and an unknown drawing of a girl standing on a cliff. From where did they come?

Sybil was 22 years old and had no friends because she was ashamed about "losing time." Days would disappear that she could not recall. She realized only a psychiatrist could help her.

Her psychiatrist, Dr. Wilbur, helped Sybil recover lost moments of time. Together they discovered an amazing story. Sybil was a multiple personality. Within Sybil were 16 personalities who were struggling to survive!

Staples, Suzanne Fisher. **Haveli.** Random House, 1993, 320pp. Grades 9 & Up. Includes glossary and pronunciation guide. Second in a series: **Shabanu: Daughter of the Wind** follows.

Realistic fiction. *Abuse; India and Pakistan; sex and sexuality; women's issues.*

 This well-written sequel to **Shabanu: Daughter of the Wind** *contains some frank discussions on birth control.*

I am Shabanu, daughter of the wind. My family is nomadic and lives in the desert. I left my family to become the fourth wife of Rahim. All the other wives are jealous because I am Rahim's favorite.

These wives have tried to harm my five-year-old daughter, Mumtaz, and me. They have placed a scorpion in my bed and a rabid bat in the cupboard. I have told Rahim, and he rages at the wives, but the abuse continues. Now I hear they plan to train my daughter as a servant. This I can never permit.

Also, my best friend, Zabo, is being forced to marry the dimwitted son of my husband. This is intolerable both to me and to Zabo. We have no choice. We must escape to safety. My friend Omar has promised to help.

Where will our destiny and fate lead us?

Sweeney, Joyce. **Center Line.** Delacorte, 1984, 246pp. Grades 9 & Up.

Realistic fiction. *Abuse; men's issues; runaways; sex and sexuality; substance abuse (alcohol and drugs).*

We had to leave home. Dad was becoming more abusive every day, and, since Mom was killed in a car accident, we had no protection. One day Dad would kill us.

I'm Shawn, 18 years old and the oldest of five brothers. I made a decision that would forever change our lives. We stole Dad's car and ran away to Indiana, Michigan, and Florida.

We had many adventures—some funny and some horrific. However, we learned one important lesson that we never learned in school—how to survive.

Sweeney, Joyce. **Shadow.** Delacorte, 1994, 216pp. Grades 9 & Up.

Realistic fiction. *Occult; revenge; rivalry; sex and sexuality; substance abuse (alcohol); supernatural.*

 Note: This book contains explicit language and one fairly frank sexual scene.

My cat, Shadow, is still alive, or at least her spirit is still around. I can feel her presence–her shadow.

My dad thinks I'm nuts for thinking about my dead cat. Our new Southern housekeeper, Cissy, can feel Shadow's presence, too. She even promises to conduct a seance to find out why Shadow's spirit is coming around.

Cissy and I believe Shadow is bringing my family a warning of some disaster. Could it have to do with my brothers, Brian and Patrick, fighting over the same girl?

Tamar, Erika. **Fair Game.** Harcourt, Brace, 1993, 293pp. Grades 9 & Up.

Realistic fiction. *Crime; disability (mental); ethics; men's issues; sexual abuse.*

Note: The girl who is the subject of Laura's letter is mentally impaired and incapable of making wise judgments. This excellent book is about assuming responsibility.

Dear Editor:

I am writing to protest the articles about the high school athletes of Shorehaven. I've known these boys for a long time and have gone to school with them all my life. They didn't commit any crime. Why did you print their pictures with the headline "Jock Assault"? I thought this was America, where they are innocent until proven guilty.

Everyone knows the girl was available to anybody and that she'd been servicing half the football team. What happened that day was her choice. Even her mother doesn't want to press charges. Why didn't you list the girl's name?

Yours in justice,
Laura Jean Kettering
P.S. If you want the true story, read *Fair Game* by Erika Tamar.

Tan, Amy. **The Joy Luck Club.** G. P. Putnam's Sons, 1989, 288pp. Grades 9 & Up.

Realistic fiction. *Asian Americans; China; movie novels; rivalry; sexual abuse; women's issues.*

My father asked me to be the fourth corner of the Joy Luck Club. I am to replace my mother, who died two months ago. The Joy Luck Club was started by my mother in San Francisco in 1949, two years before I was born. The idea originated with my mother during her first marriage in China, before the Japanese came.

My mother wanted a gathering of four women, one for each corner of her mah jong table. Each week they would host a party with wonderful food. After a very serious game of mah jong, they would gather for stories.

Oh, what wonderful stories! Some stories were tragic, many were humorous, all were entertaining. There were stories of arranged marriages, thoughtless daughters, obedient mothers.

By accepting my mother's place at the fourth corner of the Joy Luck Club, I learned a secret she kept locked in her heart. I traveled to China to meet my sisters that my mother left behind so many years ago.

Now I understand my mother in a way I never did when she was alive.

Thomas, Rob. **Rats Saw God.** Simon & Schuster for Young People, 1996, 219pp.; (Pbk.) Aladdin Paperback, 1997, 219pp. Grades 9 & Up. An ALA Best Books for Young Adults selection.

Realistic fiction. *Men's issues; sex and sexuality; substance abuse.*

I've been told that I'm gifted. I'm also bored and stoned most of the time.

In one semester alone I've tallied one "possession" charge and three "under the influence" charges. I made 760 on my verbal SATs and failed English. I "transferred" from a preppy Houston school by walking out of class, getting into my El Camino car and driving 27 hours non-stop to California. My mom was living there with her new husband. He's a guy she enjoys playing tongue hockey with.

This New Age school psychologist swears my problems are tied in with my dad being a world famous astronaut. He thinks I'm "acting out" my rebellion. No way. I happen to like looking like a pirate with my two hoop earrings and doo rag.

This psychologist insists I write on any topic I like. All the experts say to write about what you know. Well, I'm an authority on my life.

So join me on my X-rated tour through the backroads of my mind.

Twain, Mark. **The Adventures of Tom Sawyer.** Penguin Books, 1994, 282pp. First published in 1876. For all ages.

Historical fiction. *Men's issues; movie novels; rites of passage; school.*

Note: Tom's friend continues the story in **Huckleberry Finn.** *Many think the book is racist because of the character Jim, a runaway slave.*

Tarnation, that Tom Sawyer will be the death of me. I'm his Aunt Polly and trying to do my duty by raising that boy for my dead sister. Hang the boy, I can't keep up with him. He's up to his tricks every single day, so how is a body to know what's coming?

Like the time Tom, Huckleberry Finn, and Joe Harper ran away to become pirates. Had a grand old time, too. 'Bout worried me senseless.

He and his buddies also searched for buried treasure, sneaked into a haunted house, and hung around a graveyard at midnight. Once, they showed up at their own funeral!

Thinking about all his foolishness has got me in such a state. I got to end my tirade. I'll let you find out for yourself what a rascal that Tom Sawyer is.

Walker, Kate. **Peter.** Houghton Mifflin, 1991, 170pp. Grades 9 & Up.

Realistic fiction. *Homosexuality; men's issues; sex and sexuality; sports (dirt bike riding).*

Note: *Don't miss this excellent page-turner by Australian writer Kate Walker. Many important issues about masculinity are discussed.*

I'm confused.

I'm 15, not bad looking, and pretty athletic, especially on my dirt bike. My buddies and me also like talking about and looking at girls. Then I meet my older brother's friend, David, and--well, I'm confused.

See, David's gay. I have trouble thinking or saying that word. I know lots of other words and have used them many times, especially around my buddies. Then I meet David and all those stereotypes go right outta my head. David is different from what I thought a gay guy would be. He's funny, brilliant, nice to be around. Like, normal, actually.

See why I'm confused?

Webster, Jean. **Daddy Long-Legs.**
Puffin Books, 1989, 185pp. First
published in 1912. For all ages.

Romance. *Europe (France); love; movie
novels; orphans; rites of passage.*

Dear Daddy Long-Legs,

It's strange writing to someone I don't know. Still, that is our
agreement. You will pay for my college as a faceless benefactor; I
will write to you monthly, calling you Mr. John Smith.

I don't like the name John Smith. That name seems so imper-
sonal. Besides, you are not entirely unknown to me. I did see your
shadow once. You were very tall, so I will respectfully call you
Daddy Long-Legs.

I love college and am never homesick. How can I be homesick
for an orphan asylum?

It's very possible I could fall in love with you. I know you are
too busy to answer my letters, but I have to know: Are you married?

Faithfully yours,

Jerusha (Judy) Abbott

Wein, Elizabeth E. **The Winter
Prince.** Atheneum, 1993, 202pp.
Grades 9 & Up.

Folklore. *Great Britain; magic; occult;
revenge; rivalry; sex and sexuality;
sexual abuse; supernatural.*

Note: *This book is another
fractured fairy tale that
tells a believable story
of revenge. It could be used with
books by Robin McKinley (on page
83) and Donna Jo Napoli (page
124). It mentions incest and
illegitimacy.*

I am Medraught, also known as Mordred, King Arthur's illegit-
imate son. Of course, I am not the designated heir to the throne.
No, my younger half-brother, Lleu, will assume that role.

That I can accept with dignity. What I can not accept is the
Prince's public taunting of my deepest, darkest secret. My mother and father are brother and sister. That treachery I can never
forgive!

Now I will do all I can to destroy the Prince—even if I destroy
myself in the process!

Wells, H. G. **The Time Machine.**
Edited by John Lawton. J. M.
Dent/Everyman's Library, 1997, 106pp.
First published in 1895. Grades 8 & Up.

Science fiction. *Class conflict; end-of-the-world; movie novels; science; survival; time travel.*

 This was H. G. Wells's first novel and it became an instant classic. Wells was familiar with Darwin's theory of evolution and used his scientific knowledge to produce a horrifying vision of the future. Recommend this one to readers who think they don't like science fiction.

"Upon this machine," said the Time Traveler to us scholars, "I intend to explore time."

I don't think any of us believed him. However, the next Thursday we all gathered at the Time Traveler's house as usual, but we were instructed to begin dinner if he hadn't arrived by the appointed hour. Imagine our shock when the Time Traveler staggered in. He agreed to tell us of his amazing journey through time to the year 802,701.

His excursion revealed two human civilizations: one lived above the ground; the other, underground. The Eloi lived on Earth, which looked like a paradise; they were fair and beautiful, but weak minded. The Morlocks lived underground and were hideous creatures who feared light. Sadly, the Eloi were merely fatted cattle for the hideous Morlocks. Literally! The Morlocks were cannibals!

Take a trip into this time machine.

Woodson, Jacqueline. **From the Notebooks of Melanin Sun.** Blue Sky/Scholastic, 1995, 141pp. Grades 9 & Up. An ALA Best Books for Young Adults selection.

Realistic fiction. *African Americans; homosexuality; interracial relations; sex and sexuality.*

 Jacqueline Woodson is a brilliant writer, but her themes and characters are controversial. This one is about an interracial relationship between two women. Read this one before you recommend it to others.

My name is Melanin Sun. According to Mama, I am dark like melanin, a pigment, and I'm like the sun at the same time. Go figure. I wish my name were David.

I wish I weren't so different from everyone. I feel like a Peeping Tom, always on the outside looking in. I wish it didn't matter so much, being different from everyone. But it does, doesn't it? Difference matters.

I've got a different kind of problem than most. Mama's in love--again. This time she's gone too far for my taste. In love with Kristin, a white chick!

Anyway, these are my notebooks. My stories. Secrets. Skeletons. I keep quiet. Watch. And write it all down.

Woodson, Jacqueline. **I Hadn't Meant to Tell You This.** Delacorte, 1994, 115pp. Grades 9 & Up. An ALA Best Books for Young Adults selection.

Realistic fiction. *African Americans; interracial relations; problem parents; runaways; secrets; sexual abuse.*

 *This well-written book is about incest.*

I hadn't meant to tell you this. I promised Lena I would never tell. Crossed my heart and hoped to die if I ever told.

Last night I had a dream. When I woke up, I knew it was okay to tell. It seemed like Lena was saying, "It's okay now, Marie. Go ahead and tell it. Then maybe someday other girls like you and me can live in this crazy world without being afraid."

So I will start at the beginning and tell the whole world.

This one's for you, Lena.

The Latest and Greatest: Booktalking the Best-Sellers (Grades 9 & Up)

The following is a presentation of booktalks. These books have been on the New York Times best-sellers list within the last five years and are enjoyable reads. A few have the makings of modern classics. All are entertaining and informative.

These booktalks are not contained elsewhere in this book. They are included within all the indexes, however, so you can use them with all the other booktalks. Photocopy them just as you would the other booktalks in this book.

These booktalks are designed for high school students, teachers, librarians, book discussion groups, or parent-teacher organizations. Selected middle school readers may enjoy them, too.

While booktalking best-sellers, your book selection will change each time. Of course, your introduction will vary, as well. Generally, people like to hear about the latest best-sellers, novels that are turned into recent films, and Oprah Winfrey's book selections. You might mention a recent article or television program that relates to the book. Then continue into your selected books. Multiple copies of the books and audiotapes should be available and presented during the talk. You might begin your presentation this way:

Many current best-sellers are compelling reads. Recently the boundaries between fiction and nonfiction have blurred. A nonfiction book can read like an adventure thriller. A novel can replicate the style of a memoir. Even an autobiography can read like pulp fiction.

For example, the best-seller ***Into Thin Air: A Personal Account of the Mount Everest Disaster*** (Anchor/Doubleday, 1998) reads like Jack London's fiction. This story, however, is factual:

On May 10, 1996, nine climbers died on a guided ascent to Mount Everest. Within the next months three more climbers died. Why did veteran Himalayan guides and their inexperienced climbers keep ascending the mountain with a deadly storm brewing?

Nobody can speak for the leaders of the two guided groups because both men are dead. However, I, Jon Krakauer, was there as a writer and climber. I don't recall seeing threatening clouds. Of course, it is hard to be alert when your brain is depleted of oxygen.

Since I've returned, I've gone over the details repeatedly. The Everest climb rocked my life to its core. Some spent $65,000 apiece to be taken safely up Everest. Instead, multiple tragedies occurred.

What happened? I will take you through our climb, step by step.

Read **Into Thin Air: A Personal Account of the Mount Everest Disaster, by Jon Krakauer.**

This next book reads like a memoir or nonfiction. According to *Book* magazine, this novel is a favorite among book discussion groups:

I'm Nitta Sayuri. Writers have called me one of the greatest geisha of Kyoto. I assure you that I was never the greatest geisha. Yet my story twists and turns like the Sea of Japan, beginning in the fishing village of Yoroido.

My sign is water. Water never waits. Water changes shape and flows around things and finds secret paths. When Mr. Tanaka persuaded my father to live with him in Senzuru, I began my journey. My destiny was changed forever.

Mr. Tanaka took me to an okiya, a place where geisha live, and sold me. I began as a servant and was subject to beatings and abuse.

The head geisha, Hatsumomo, was particularly cruel. She accused me of stealing money and of pouring ink on her rival's kimono. Luckily, her rival, Mameha, knew I had not damaged her kimono and began training me as her apprentice. Perhaps she wanted revenge on her rival.

Like water, I began to adapt to my surroundings. I learned the dances, the music, the makeup, and the art of making my customers satisfied. I became what dreams are made of.

My dream is only about one man, called

the Chairman. He was the only person kind to me during my years of torment. Can the Chairman rescue me from the life I never chose, the life of a geisha?

Find out in **Memoirs of a Geisha, by Arthur Golden.**

Memoirs of a Geisha will become a movie produced by Steven Spielberg.

One book that will never become a film is *Catcher in the Rye*. Its author, J. D. Salinger, refuses to sell the movie rights. Currently, Salinger is in the media spotlight again after being reclusive for decades. Joyce Maynard has written extensively of her relationship with him in *At Home in the World* (St. Martin's, 1998):

J. D. Salinger wrote Catcher in the Rye *in 1951 to great acclaim. Shortly afterward he disappeared from the literary scene. He has not published anything in more than 30 years. His personal life has been private. Until now.*

Joyce Maynard had a brief but intense relationship with Salinger during 1973. After their breakup, Maynard continued to write autobiographical pieces about her marriage and children. Maynard never referred to Salinger. Until now.

Who is J. D. Salinger? What did he become? Why did he retreat from the world? What did the 39-year-old writer see in a girl of 18? Reportedly, Salinger is furious at the intrusion of his privacy. But, as Maynard protests, "This is my story, too."

For her story, read **Joyce Maynard's** *revealing memoir,* **At Home in the World.**

Sometimes a memoir can be as entertaining as a story told around a fire. Songwriter and singer Jimmy Buffet writes a breezy account of his adventures at sea and on the Caribbean islands:

I'm Jimmy Buffet: musician, songwriter,

pilot, world traveler, philosopher. My philosophy? Follow your instincts and keep a sense of humor.

Sometimes it's hard to laugh. Once I flipped over my seaplane in the Atlantic Ocean. That wasn't funny. Neither were the stitches in my skull from surfing in the Gulf during a hurricane. But I'm known to take a risk or two.

I'll admit it. I'm a pirate. By nature, I am a creature of the swamps and the sea. I enjoy the adventure of life on the sea.

I hope you'll enjoy the ride in **A Pirate Looks at Fifty, by Jimmy Buffet.**

The sea can bring disaster as well. The sinking of the Titanic in 1912 was proof of that. When James Cameron released his movie *Titanic*, he had tapped into a timeless story. The movie inspired a cult of followers. Journalist Paula Paris tells a fascinating story of the making of the movie, the discovery of the wreck, and, yes, even the contribution of Leonardo DiCaprio.

The movie Titanic was the first to gross more than one billion dollars worldwide and to win 11 Academy Awards. The story behind the movie is just as fascinating as the movie.

Director James Cameron took more than three years to write and direct the film. He even went on underwater dives to the ship-wrecked Titanic. The footage you see during the first minutes of the movie was taken during Cameron's expedition.

There were many problems during the filming. Once the movie set plunged five feet, and water rushed onto the deck. That day the set became almost as tragic as the real Titanic.

Casting the roles was a problem, too. At first the director didn't want Leonardo DiCaprio in the role of Jack. Cameron wanted an actor like Tom Cruise. Actor Kate Winslet wasn't Cameron's first choice, either. After she auditioned, she told the director, "You don't have to choose me for Rose, but you've got to

hire Leonardo." How right she was.

For the inside story of the movie read **Titanic and the Making of James Cameron, by Paula Paris.**

Another media event was the shocking death of Princess Diana. So much of what has been written about her life reads as pulp fiction. Perhaps the most balanced account of her life is by someone who knew her personally:

Who was the real Princess Diana? Was she Shy Di or a Plastic Princess? A naive young girl, or a manipulative media teaser? Diana was all these things and more. Diana was more complex and complicated than her public ever suspected.

The author knew both Diana and Charles before and after their marriage. Their romance and divorce had been reported on by many outsiders, but the author was a constant participant and observer of the social and royal scene.

Here is Princess Diana: clever, childlike, cunning, and canny.

Here is **The Real Diana, by Lady Colin Campbell.**

Many years ago another tragedy was exploited in the media. In 1930 Charles Lindbergh's infant son was stolen from his nursery and murdered. This media event drew as much attention in its time as Princess Diana's death did in ours. Charles Lindbergh and Anne Morrow Lindbergh raised five more children. Their eldest daughter, Reeve, tells of their life in *Under a Wing* (Simon & Schuster, 1998):

"This is Reeve Lindbergh. She is Charles Lindbergh's daughter, you know."

"You mean, she is Anne Morrow's daughter, of course," the firm voice corrected her.

I am both, of course. I am the daughter of pilot Charles Lindbergh and writer Anne Morrow. How was it to grow up in a family of two legends? In their time they were as famous a couple as Franklin and Eleanor Roosevelt.

Actually, it was a highly functional and supportive family. My brother was kidnapped and killed before either I was or my siblings were born. When I became an adult, I also lost my only child. My mother advised me to say goodbye to my dead child. I then realized my mother never had that opportunity during her own son's death.

Growing up, I heard the gossip that my father, Charles Lindbergh, was anti-Semitic. Once he visited Nazi Germany and publicly admired the government. Later he made a controversial speech that seemed to affirm these actions. I will try to explain the reasons why my father might have said such despicable things.

Here is the human side to two legends that only a daughter can write. Soar with **Under a Wing by Reeve Lindbergh.**

This next best-seller, a courtroom drama, reads as a mystery thriller, yet it is factual. When this book was first published in 1994, it became both a best-seller and a critical success. Its success was revived with the 1997 movie version of the story. Most people felt that the book was superior to the film. Try John Berendt's chilling *Midnight in the Garden of Good and Evil* (Random House, 1994):

I'm John Berendt, a Yankee reporter from New York.

The first time I heard about Savannah, Georgia, was in the book "Treasure Island." The bloodthirsty pirate Captain John Flint lived there.

Savannah also is mentioned in "Gone with the Wind," as a quiet, genteel Southern town.

Savannah is certainly quite on the surface and bloodthirsty underneath. I would find myself involved in an adventure that included a wide mixture of characters. They include a

drag queen, a Southern belle, a voodoo priestess, and an antiques dealer. All were somehow involved in a horrific murder.

The tragedy of this story is that all of this story is true. Read **Midnight in the Garden of Good and Evil, by John Berendt.**

Oprah Winfrey selected the next book as one of her book choices. Indian writer Arundhati Roy has written a multilayered novel in *The God of Small Things* (HarperCollins 1998):

It all began when Sophie Mol came to Ayemenem, a town in the southernmost tip of India. Sometimes a few dozen hours can affect the outcome of lifetimes. When this happens, these few dozen hours must be examined like an aging photograph. Accounted for.

Sophie Mol visited Ayemenem only for a week. She left Ayemenem in a coffin. She left her family behind in grief and bewilderment.

The twins Estha and Rahel had grown to love their cousin within that week. Sophie Mol understood their desire to be unconditionally loved by their mother, Ammu. Sophie Mol ran away with them that fateful day to demonstrate her support for their actions. That support led Sophie Mol to a watery grave.

On the other hand, perhaps the story begins during a Marxist demonstration when the Untouchable Velutha was seen by Sophie Mol's aunt.

Perhaps the story begins thousands of years ago. The Love Laws told their ancestors who were the Touchable People and the Untouchables.

Maybe it doesn't matter where or when the story begins, but how it ends and who delivers it. Therefore, this story is brought to you by **The God of Small Things. The storyteller is Arundhati Roy.**

Death is also the theme of the next novel. The character Ellen Gulden is accused of aiding in her mother's death from cancer. In the 1998 movie, actress Meryl Streep plays the dying mother in Anna Quindlen's *One True Thing* (Bantam Doubleday Dell, 1997):

> *I know what the police, the newspapers, the lawyers and my family are saying. They are wrong. I did not kill my mother. I just wish I had.*
>
> *I guess everyone feels I betrayed them. I left my hometown for fame and glory as a journalist. I returned only to help my mother cope with her death sentence of cancer. I never dreamed that I was helping to end my own life.*
>
> *So I guess I did kill someone. I killed that heartless and superficial part of myself that longed to be everything my mother wasn't. For I learned that my mother represented the one true thing that mattered–love.*

> *Read* **One True Thing***, by Anna Quindlen.*

Sidda also had a complex relationship with her mother. Her mother appeared to care more for her group of rabble-rousing girl-friends, the Ya-Yas:

> *Sidda received a thick package from her estranged mother. Inside were a letter and a brown leather scrapbook, stuffed with letters and photographs. The letter said:*
>
> *Sidda,*
>
> *What do you mean you "don't know how to love"? Good God, child, who does? Only God knows. The rest of us are acting.*
>
> *Your mother,*
>
> *Vivi Abbott Walker*
>
> *P.S. I'm sending you the "Divine Secrets of the Ya-Yas." Don't think I've told all my secrets. I have others.*
>
> *Sidda gingerly opened the scrapbook, truly honored that her mother would share this treasure. The yellowed pages exposed a 50-year friendship among four women who called themselves the Ya-Yas.*
>
> *The Ya-Yas had opinions about everything. Something great was "Ya-Ya." Like the time the four went skinny-dipping in the town's water tank at midnight, Ya-Ya. When they were arrest-*

ed and booked for a night in jail, Ya-Ya-No!

> *Maybe the scrapbook can help Sidda recover from her mid-life depression. Your spirits will definitely soar at these outrageous women who run with the wolves. Read* **Divine Siecrets of the Ya-Ya Sisterhood***, by Rebecca Wells. Ya-Ya!*

In conclusion, all of these best-sellers will grab your interest. They all tell a compelling story, whether it's fact or fiction. See if you can tell the difference between the two. Check them out!

Author Index

[T]itle Index

Genre Index

You can choose a genre and have a quick list of recommended books:

NONFICTION

POETRY

REALISTIC FICTION

ROMANCE

SCIENCE FICTION

SHORT STORIES

SPORTS

Selected Subject Index

These subjects may be helpful for your booktalks. Pick a theme or country and find a list of recommended books. Most books can fit into several different categories and, therefore, can be approached from a variety of different ways.

MIDDLE AGES

MIDDLE EAST

MOVIE NOVELS

MUSIC

NATIVE AMERICANS

OCCULT

SURVIVAL

TIME TRAVEL

TRUST

Genres and Subjects for Booktalks

▶ GENRES

Adventure

Biography

Fantasy

Folklore

Historical Fiction

Horror

Humor

Mysteries/Thrillers

Nonfiction

Poetry

Realistic Fiction

Romance

Science Fiction

Sports

Short Stories

▶ SUBJECTS

Abuse

Aging

Adoption

Africa

African Americans

AIDS

American Revolutionary War

Animals

Apartheid

Asia

Asian Americans

Caribbean and Latin America

China

Class Conflict

Civil War, 1860-1865

Computers

Crime

Death

Diaries

Disability

Divorce

Eating Disorders

Ecology

End-of-the-World

Ethics

Europe

Family

Friendship

Great Britain

Hispanic Americans

Hobbies

Holocaust

Homeless

Homosexuality

Illness

Immigrants

India

Interracial Relations

Ireland

Jews

Love

Magic

Men's Issues

Middle Ages

Middle East

Movie Novels

Music

Native Americans

Occult

Orphans

Peer Pressure

Pioneer Life

Politics

Pregnancy

Problem Parents

Racism

Religion

Religious Prejudice

Responsibility

Revenge

Rites of Passage

Rivalry

Runaways

School

Science

Secrets

Self-identity

Sex and Sexuality

Sexual Abuse

Show Business

Single Parents

South Africa

Sports

Stepparents

Substance Abuse

Suicide

Supernatural

Survival

Time Travel

Trust

Vietnam War

War

World War I

World War II

Women's issues

Work